DATE DUE

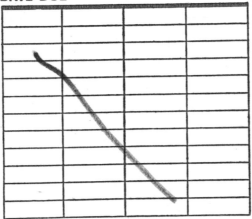

American Higher Education
1945–1970

American Higher Education
1945-1970

A Personal Report

Nathan M. Pusey

Harvard University Press

Cambridge, Massachusetts, and London, England

1978

Copyright © 1978 by the President and Fellows of Harvard College
All rights reserved
Printed in the United States of America

Library of Congress Cataloging in Publication Data

Pusey, Nathan Marsh, 1907–
    American higher education, 1945–1970.

    1.   Education, Higher—United States—History.
I.   Title.
LA226.P95   378.73   77–16066
ISBN 0–674–02425–7

For the Fellows of Harvard College,
members of the Board of Overseers,
and the Deans of Harvard's several faculties
who served in my time

Contents

Introduction   1

1. The New Worldwide Perspectives   15

2. Graduate Education and Research
   Capability   46

3. Finances   89

4. Conflicts   123

5. Aims   160

American Higher Education
1945–1970

Introduction

It is the argument of this book that the quarter-century from 1945 to 1970 constituted a definable and notable period in the history of higher education in the United States.

The period, which was to prove a time of extraordinarily rich opportunity, began with the end of the Second World War, when the colleges and universities returned, eagerly and optimistically, following the disruptions caused them by the war, to their normal pursuits. It ended in or about 1970 with the institutions of higher education facing a sharp decline in public favor, the prospect of shrinking enrollments, an impending end to growth, intensified financial difficulties, the need for retrenchment, and increasing government regulation. And, if these vicissitudes were not in themselves sufficient to signal the beginning of a new period, it can be added that they occurred at a time when morale within the academic profession had been seriously impaired by the unsettling disturbances which erupted on

campuses in the late 1960s and the frequently in-
judicious responses which were made to them.

My small book endeavors to give an account of the
dramatic development achieved by higher education
during that period. I say "achieved," though perhaps
"occurred" would be a more accurate word. College
presidents, called on relentlessly to make a public case
for their institutions, usually assert that colleges and
universities are the creative leaders of society. They
were established and are maintained, they proclaim, to
engender and support quality in the lives of individuals
and in our nation, and they are organized and equipped
as no other of our agencies are to accomplish this purpose. In the more elevated of their rhetorical flourishes
they speak of them as the bellwethers of our country's
social, economic, and cultural advance. There is considerable justification for such claims, but in more
candid moments, on less public occasions, these same
presidents will sometimes acknowledge that their institutions frequently react to developments rather than
initiate and lead them. Certainly this was true during
most of the years between 1945 and 1970, when the
academic world was kept busy in a continuous effort to
keep up with the pace of change.

The Second World War created a quite new set of
circumstances for our national life. The country's industrial capacity and economic might were enormously increased during these years. Toward their close there began a sudden and continuing sharp rise in population.
The interests of American citizens were lifted beyond

their own shores—even beyond Europe. Such developments could not fail to affect higher education; and in the years that followed, as the United States assumed responsibility for leadership of the free world and found itself a superpower engaged in endless and costly contention with a rival, totalitarian superpower, the country was launched on a new creative period of economic growth, worldwide responsibility, and scientific and technical advance that continued to influence profoundly the development of its academic life.

The nation's colleges and universities had devoted much of their energy during the war years toward helping to meet the country's extraordinary military, training, and health needs. This involvement in practical affairs accelerated in the postwar years. Interest in the institutions of higher education and in their activities spread to more elements of the population; as this occurred more and more individuals and groups of individuals came to look expectantly—and with mounting impatience—to what came to be called "the knowledge industry" for solutions to a vast range of society's problems. In this time of almost continuous economic growth, with the nation seeking to discharge worldwide responsibility, higher education came to seem indispensable to, indeed almost the very life blood of, the huge, complicated, urban, technological, industrial, managerial society that had developed and was expanding in America.

This heightened expectation exerted a continuous pressure on the institutions of higher education to grow, to expand and develop their traditional activities, and to accept new responsibilities. International considerations were given increased prominence in old and new curricula in both colleges and universities as their interests were expanded to encompass the whole world. New interdisciplinary area studies were devised to explore and teach about countries, regions, and peoples that had earlier been largely ignored. Students and faculty were recruited on a worldwide basis. To keep pace with accelerating demands for new knowledge and more highly trained talent constantly arising in both public and private sectors of society, graduate study and research activity increased in universities far beyond any earlier anticipation. The upper reaches of the known were repeatedly extended, as incentives for research— and, more important, support for it—continued unabated from numerous sources. Research techniques became more and more sophisticated. Fields of investigation divided and subdivided. Scholarly publication flourished. Scholarly journals multiplied throughout the world (there were approximately 40,000 of them by the period's end). Academic life was enriched and made more attractive, and the country's intellectual resources were handsomely augmented as ever-larger numbers of qualified scholars in field after field, including many new fields were trained at home or recruited from abroad.

Midway in this period I published a book suggesting that the age of the scholar had arrived. Perhaps I should have said, the age of the research scholar. But in any event there can be no doubt that during this twenty-five-year period, in response to the demands made upon them and the opportunities presented to them, the nation's universities grew in number, in the reach and variety of their interests, and in their intellectual and physical resources. Advances made by the colleges in their sphere of activity—curricular and, perhaps even more important, the environment for undergraduate learning—were no less conspicuous or significant. Higher education in America, with all its recognized shortcomings and blemishes, responding creatively to the many challenges it confronted during these years, had reached a new level of competence and appreciation and had grown into a position of unchallenged prominence in the world.

The quantitative changes are the most readily observable. The great physical expansion that occurred is all the more remarkable when one recalls that in the years immediately preceding the war many knowledgeable individuals had persuaded themselves that the period of growth in America was coming to an end and that enrollment in the institutions of higher education had nearly reached the upper level that could be expected. Student population in the last "normal" year before the war had reached what was then considered the very high level of 1.4 million. It had not surprisingly suffered a sharp decline during the war years as young men volunteered for or were drafted into military service. But with the demobilization of the veterans, which began in late 1945, it rose in less than a year and a half to exceed the

earlier high figure by more than a million. It fell off a
few years later, roughly around 1950, after the full tide
of veterans had passed through and as the outbreak of
the Korean War posed a new threat. Soon, however,
with a rapidly growing national population and increased desire on the part of the young to attend college,
the upward surge began again and continued thereafter
in considerably greater degree than anyone had anticipated, until by 1970 more than 8 million students,
nearly 50 percent of the relevant age group, were enrolled in the nation's colleges and universities. It seems
to me that this great expansion, representing a number
and a percentage never previously even remotely approached anywhere in the world, by itself would justify
the application of the adjective "notable" to this period
in the history of higher education.

The case does not rest on this fact alone. There were
many qualitative changes. One need only compare the
number and range of courses offered by any college or
university in 1970 with those offered in 1940 to gain an
indication of the impressive expansion of intellectual
interest that occurred. I shall have considerably more to
say about this; but at this point let me offer a few additional figures to flesh out the indication of quantitative
advance. In 1940 there were 1,750 colleges and universities in the United States. These were staffed by
132,000 faculty and administrative officers, of whom
110,000 did the teaching. By 1970 the number of institutions had increased by more than a thousand to reach
the figure of 2,850, and there were nearly 500,000

faculty members conducting residential degree programs. The preparation of this number of teachers was itself a remarkable achievement. It is also worth noting that much of the increase being suggested here occurred at the upper reaches of the enterprise, at the level of what in earlier years I often referred to as the "higher higher education." Here, only two more statistics: The expense of operating the enterprise of higher education rose from $600 million in 1940 to $24 billion in 1970. Somehow year by year these sums were found, and along with them capital funds through which the value of the institutions' physical facilities grew—largely because of new construction, if also in part because of inflation—from $2.75 billion to $42 billion.

The colleges and universities of the United States enjoyed public favor and experienced stimuli and opportunity for growth and development between 1945 and 1970 beyond anything they had known earlier. All of them prospered, and some of the larger ones grew in strength and range of interest to become the most highly advanced institutions for learning yet achieved anywhere in the world. This rapid development tended to raise private and public expectations concerning what they could do and to confront them with many new, and some would say, highly questionable, demands for a variety of services. But though doubts were sometimes expressed, and questions raised about the proper purpose of higher education and the quality of current practice, it was a remarkably favorable period for higher education, and on the whole its path continued steadily upward. It was accorded generous financial support—most significantly, after much hesitation and debate, in large amounts, especially for research, by the federal government. Until the very end of the period the prevailing mood within academic circles was happily optimistic. It seemed to me at the time, as it does now, that viewed in its entirety the pluses brought about by the changes far outweighed the minuses, that it was a uniquely fortunate period for higher education, and one of such extensive and remarkable achievement as to entitle it to be considered one of the most creative our country has yet experienced.

It was my good fortune, from earlier experience in college teaching, to have had a part in academic administration during the whole of this period, first as president of a college of liberal arts, and then, from 1953, as president of one of the nation's leading research universities. I put down my impressions of some of what I consider to have been the more important developments that took place in higher education during these years in an effort to contribute to a clearer understanding of an exceptionally productive but as yet imperfectly interpreted period. I have wanted to do this because in my judgment the very considerable accomplishments of the period, well known to those of us who participated in them, were not only distorted but largely obscured, if not obliterated, for a wider public by the intense attention that was focused on the campus disturbances that marred its closing years. It is my conviction—or at least my hope—that if one will look again, fairly, at what went on in colleges and universities during these years, the period will be seen, not as one best neglected and forgotten, but rather as one to be remembered happily and gratefully, perhaps even to be celebrated.

Before proceeding, let me say a few words about the beginning of the period. The months immediately preceding the opening of the school year in the autumn of 1945 had brought increased anxiety to college and university administrative officers and trustees. Those associated with privately controlled institutions had special cause to worry, for almost all of these institutions were, as they continue to be, heavily dependent on income from tuition to keep alive. For them, along with more admirable considerations, students mean dollars; and with the closing of the military programs that had brought succor to many of them, and an anticipated college and university enrollment for the coming year for the whole country of no more than 800,000 students, the prospect for all of these institutions was grim. But the gloom was swept away in an eruption of eager expectation before the end of August, as the war ended and it became clear that the demobilization would soon begin.

Enrollments began to swell before the end of the first semester. They increased more rapidly in the spring. By the following autumn, thanks to the financial provisions of the G.I. Bill of Rights, more than a million veterans were enrolled, and more would follow. Though there is never an absence of problems for administrative officers to struggle with, they do change. Certainly they did here, for worries about having too few students to pay the tuitions needed to balance budgets were soon succeeded by unanticipated and very urgent needs to make place for the multitudes of students who swarmed onto the campuses and to find qualified teachers to teach them. Double- and triple-deck beds were installed in existing dormitories, and Quonset huts and barrack units made available by the federal government were erected to provide additional student rooms, classrooms, and faculty offices. Retired teachers, faculty wives, and individuals with various degrees of professional training from other walks of life were pressed into service to meet the need for additional instructors. These were real problems, but after years of anxiety occasioned by relentless and seemingly insoluble financial pressures, they constituted a relatively pleasant kind of worry.

There was, however, considerable initial anxiety on the part of faculty members concerning how the veterans were to be handled. They had had very little experience dealing with undergraduate students of the veterans' ages, and none with students who had piloted airplanes over great distances, had shot and been shot at, and had been subjected to many exacting tests and to experiences totally unknown to most of the teachers. These individuals were understandably worried about how such students would react to college environments, to the available curricular offerings, and to their teaching. Their worries quickly evaporated, however, as the veterans, confident of what formal education could do for them both personally and professionally and eager to make up for lost time and get on with their careers. revealed unprecedented enthusiasm for learning. With few exceptions they applied themselves to their studies, exhibited mature behavior in the academic environment, and brought more mature concerns to it than had ever previously been witnessed there. They were genuinely and deeply interested in the subjects of their courses, quick to contribute to classroom discussions, and searching and persistent in questioning everything their teachers had to say. Beyond this they brought into what had been relatively sheltered academic communities experiences and knowledge of distant parts of the world that had earlier been given little attention there, but which were henceforth to be of increasing importance in academic curricula and in the nation's life.

There followed for a few years an unusual and memorable period in higher education. If one overlooks the labor disputes that broke out almost immediately after the war years, during which strikes had been prohibited, this was for a short time a euphoric period for the whole country. There was happiness about—rejoicing in victory, and renewed faith in democracy. In popular understanding the war had been brought about by the threat posed to democracies by the rise of Hitlerism in Germany, and it had been won. Democracy had been vindicated, its superiority demonstrated. There was reason to exult, and not least in the colleges and universities, for they were justifiably proud of the contribution they had made to the happy result by providing expert knowledge of many kinds, by conducting research and training programs to assist the war effort, and, not least, by the personal service of many of their members. On top of all this, for a brief moment one could imagine that an era of universal peace had been secured.

Numerous members of faculties who taught graduate courses during these years, for whom the production of scholars is a major concern, and others who taught advanced students in professional schools, have frequently said in my hearing that the students they had in their classes at that time were the best, the most stimulating, and the most rewarding they have ever taught. The claim is made credible by the subsequent careers of many of the students, not least by the numbers of individuals who have recently risen to prominence in academic life whose graduate training dates from those years. I can testify from my own experience that teaching undergraduates—those of normal college age mixed with the larger numbers of veterans with their greater age and wider experience—was extraordinarily exciting. I have mentioned the increased eagerness and seriousness the veterans brought to the classroom, but their influence was no less marked in other aspects of the collegiate experience. With their coming, campus life erupted with unprecedented vigor. Their interest, energy, and zest introduced a new standard and enrichment into undergraduate activities, old and new. This was to persist and grow, and having thus been started, over time led to such advance and expansion in student interest and participation in theater, music, dance, art, creative writing, and athletics, too, as these were performed and enjoyed by large numbers of students in the 1950s and early 1960s, as to effect a virtual transformation of undergraduate life.

It was a happy, creative, and exciting period, and even college presidents could enjoy it; for after long drought, for a moment at least, nearly every college and university in the country found mature and able students in plentiful supply.

1

+O+O+O+O+O+O

The New Worldwide
Perspectives

Nothing is more noteworthy in the remarkable development that took place in higher education in the post–
World War II period than the extent to which its teaching and research interests were expanded to encompass
the whole world. In the aftermath of the First World
War, in which the United States first fought with others
in an attempt to make the world safe for democracy, the
country's voters repudiated President Wilson's leadership and drew back from international involvement.
This time the mood was entirely different. We were
eagerly and expectantly in the world to stay, and because of this a wholly new and exciting prospect and
responsibility opened for higher education.

The lend lease arrangements for military purposes
that had existed between our country and a number of
foreign governments from the early war years were
quickly replaced, and extended, at the war's end by
programs of aid for relief and for the rehabilitation of
devastated areas to stimulate economic recovery. The
Truman Doctrine calling for assistance to war-torn

Europe, enunciated by General Marshall at the Harvard Commencement in 1947, led to passage by Congress the next spring of the European Recovery Act, the so-called "Marshall Plan." At this point the country's attention was still chiefly directed to areas that had long been of national concern. But by 1949, following the outbreak of the Cold War, the government's perspective had broadened, and with the proclamation of President Truman's famous Point Four, the nation's international interests, including those of its colleges and universities, quickly reached beyond familiar lands to encompass all the underdeveloped, as well as the developed, countries of the world.

It began to appear that Wendell Willkie had had reason when he had spoken earlier to a doubting public about "One World," and a majority of Americans soon came to feel that it was inevitable and right that the United States should play a helpful role in the world. In fact they went further and expected their government to exercise leadership on the world stage in the interests of peace and of increased well-being for peoples everywhere. So it was not only American dollars that went abroad, but also, and in ever-increasing numbers, American people. Officers of American government and agents of American business became active throughout the world, and increasingly, with growing prosperity, Americans also traveled widely abroad for pleasure and recreation. The nation's old, endemic isolationism was ended. A new dynamic period in its history had begun. And nowhere did this vibrant new interest in all corners of the world and in international affairs flourish more vigorously than in the country's colleges and universities.

It would be incorrect to think that the interests of these institutions had ever been narrowly local. Natural scientists had always pursued their investigations without regard to political or geographical boundaries. The classics of Greece and Rome had been taught from the very beginning, along with the Bible; by the early nineteenth century the study of European languages and of modern history, if chiefly that of Western nations, had been added. By the early twentieth century most of these institutions had come also to offer courses in European diplomatic history, in international law, and in international trade. Most of these were historical in approach and devoted very little if any attention to the contemporary political, economic, or social life of the countries studied. But with the vigorous renewal of academic life that followed upon the end of the Second World War, in response to the country's new position in the world there occurred a virtual explosion of interest in international studies of all kinds, in contemporary situations as well as in historical developments, and in exotic languages and places of the world that had earlier been ignored.

This development was hastened by the curiosity and concern about distant peoples and places brought to the campuses by the veterans from their experiences abroad. It undoubtedly also owed much to the new and broadened interests that had been acquired by many members of faculties while performing service for the military, the Office of Strategic Services, or the Department of State. But the major part of the explanation for it was surely simply the wide recognition among American citizens that the United States had become a world power, that it was henceforth to be inescapably involved in worldwide responsibilities, and that this being so, they should not and could not safely remain ignorant of other peoples and cultures anywhere in the world.

An early indication of the changed attitude was the willingness of the veterans to study foreign languages and their eagerness to elect courses dealing with contemporary problems of foreign lands. Similarly indicative were the interest American students showed to pursue their studies abroad, and that shown by American colleges and universities to bring foreign students and foreign teachers to their campuses, as student and faculty exchanges with institutions in foreign countries became an established feature of American academic life. This development was made possible in large measure by Public Law 584, the "Fulbright Act," which provided the means over time for some hundred thousand Americans to study in universities in twenty countries abroad that had become our debtors during the war, and for some fifty thousand students from these countries to study here, as well as for many faculty exchanges. A private agency, The Institute of International Education, was expanded early in the postwar period to facilitate academic exchanges between the United States and other countries. And this was needed, for whereas a total of only 9,000 foreign students had been permitted to enter the United States during a five-year period before the war, by 1970 approximately 145,000 from more than eighty countries were enrolled here. The number at Harvard alone had risen from 327 in 1945 (curiously the largest number from any one country came from China) to 2,683 in 1970. Meanwhile a number of American colleges and universities had set up campuses abroad for their students, and others had joined in cooperative efforts to acquire such facilities.

Of greater and more lasting importance was the broadening effect exerted by the lively new international awareness and concern on the interests of scholars, academic curricula, fields for investigation, and the extramural activities of academic institutions. The surging interest in foreign places and international affairs swept like a wave through all the halls and all the departments of virtually all the country's colleges and universities in the early postwar years. Though this has now somewhat receded, it left a permanent enlargement in outlook and a vast enrichment of higher education in the United States, and, through its effect on generations of students, significantly altered and broadened the character of our national life by making us a less provincial people. To a degree at least, some of us have become world citizens.

The effects were felt both on undergraduate education and in every level of graduate and professional education, and even more in scholarship and research. Courses in comparative government (in the early years dealing primarily with communism, fascism, and democracy), in different economic systems, in international relations, in anthropology, and in the histories and cultures of many foreign countries were introduced or multiplied, broadened in scope, and deepened in content in colleges everywhere. More foreign languages were taught, and by the newer methods that had been devised during the war years to enable students to enter more quickly into the existing cultures of distant peoples. For example, some sixty different languages are now taught at Harvard, and, along with these, courses concerned with activities and international problems in all parts of the world are open to undergraduate students. Developments of even wider reach took place in the teaching, research and service activities at graduate levels.

Russia and the Soviet Union were among the first of the places students and faculty were eager to learn more about, and there was a rush to meet this new interest. Unfortunately, the institutions of higher education were poorly prepared for this, for in 1945 there were neither the qualified teachers nor the bibliographical resources needed. I remember the difficulty—I should say the impossibility—I experienced at that time in trying to find an American-trained scholar to teach Russian at Lawrence College. Most of those who taught in the field were emigrés from Europe, scholars of an old-world, traditional type, whose attention was directed toward the past, and who had little scholarly interest in contemporary affairs or sympathy with the newer intellectual disciplines. Only a handful of American scholars had chosen to pursue Russian studies before the war, and not all of these had taken the trouble to learn Russian. Serious exploration by American scholars of the development, organization, economics, and politics of the Soviet colossus had scarcely begun. The result was that we were ill-equipped with the specialists needed to meet the new interest and to help us as a nation to increased understanding of the wartime ally with whom we were now fated to contend for, or at least share, world power.

Harvard was initially better prepared than most other institutions to embark on an expanded program of Russian and Soviet studies, for it had long been collecting Slavic materials for its library (how foresighted were those who began this development!) and had begun to offer instruction in Slavic languages and literatures as early as 1896. About the same time it had added to its curriculum a course in Eastern European history which devoted considerable attention to Russia. Somewhat similar developments had taken place in a few other universities. I offer these few historical facts to suggest how difficult it is, how much time, planning, accumulation of materials, and training of people are required before significant advance can be attempted in any field of intellectual inquiry.

With decades of early achievement to build on, in 1948 Harvard increased its commitment to Slavic studies by establishing a fully staffed Department of Slavic Languages and Literatures, and in the same year set up its Russian Research Center. The latter, along with several similar undertakings in other universities, especially the one at Columbia, was to play a leading role in attracting and serving scholarly interest in Russian and Soviet studies. This center, the first of its kind at Harvard, provided a new kind of academic organization which enabled scholars based in different departments to work together in an association free of limiting departmental concerns in the pursuit of common interests from different points of view. This form of organization came to be used for a variety of purposes, but it would seem almost to have been a requirement for the development of area studies. A prototype for the many programs of this kind introduced at this time at Harvard and other places had been created in the Office of Strategic Services during the war years, when scholars from various academic disciplines were brought together to pool their knowledge and insights and collaborate in further investigation, to find answers to specific, urgent economic, social, geographic, and political problems relating to places in the world of strategic importance in the war effort. The practice was extraordinarily effective; it was also so stimulating to many of the participants that when they returned to their academic communities, they sought to continue and extend it. In the burgeoning new area programs they quickly found opportunities to do so.

Not all the programs in area studies set up in these years were organized in formally constituted centers, suitable as this device was for them, but whatever administrative arrangement they called forth in particular circumstances, their numbers rapidly increased, and they quickly became a conspicuous, creative, and influential feature of postwar academic life. By bringing together specialists from a variety of disciplines—humanists, social scientists, and others—to study and teach as many aspects as possible of the culture of a region, both in its historical development and in its contemporary condition, they broadened and enlivened scholarship and added a whole new dimension to academic life. They required knowledge of the language or languages used in a particular area and familiarity with its history, but they tended to attract scholars who were more interested in the present and future than in the past. They encouraged and assisted in the development of many such scholars, who in turn, through their studies and researches, added greatly to the materials needed for proper study of areas and peoples earlier neglected in American colleges and universities. Area studies were also of great value in training individuals for careers in government or in private service that required intimate knowledge of distant places. All in all, they played a role of incalculable importance in extending in universities the range of their interests, and in increasing in this country knowledge of the whole inhabited globe.

If in 1945 only a handful of American scholars knew Russian and our knowledge of the Soviet Union existed at only a very elementary level, today Russian and other Slavic languages are taught in hundreds of colleges and

universities in the United States, sophisticated investigations of all aspects of Soviet culture are conducted in
well-equipped and well-staffed (if still inadequately
supported) research centers, thousands of articles and
hundreds of books have been written adding to our
knowledge of this formidable nation and its people, and
most of those many Americans who were originally
suspicious of this development have recovered from
their early fear and misunderstanding to welcome and
be thankful for it. It is almost amusing now to remember that in the late 1940s Harvard had to disguise
the location of its Russian Research Center to prevent
zealous Red-baiters from smashing it. Meanwhile Russian and Soviet studies in the United States have grown
in sophistication to such a degree that there are now
instances on record where Americans have improved
upon the interpretations of native scholars in regard to
various aspects of Russian history and Soviet culture.
And because of the sustained effort made in a number of
our universities and colleges since the war, we have acquired impressive resources in materials and people to
continue and advance this particular work of cultural
understanding.

As a nation we were in much the same kind of weak
situation in 1945 in regard to East Asian, particularly
China, studies. There were only a very few well-qualified China scholars in the United States before the
Second World War, almost all of whom were concerned
with the literature, history, or art of China in its pre-
modern, classical periods. These were and are rich and

promising fields of unquestionable worth for study, but in themselves inadequate to meet the present national need. For China is not only the seat of an impressive ancient culture, in many ways the most impressive our planet has seen; it is also a vast, varied, contemporary nation, home of approximately a third of all the people inhabiting our world, and one with which it would seem we are destined to become increasingly involved. And yet, how little we knew—or for that matter, even now know—about it! I can testify to the fact that it was virtually impossible in the early postwar years to find a scholar of sufficient competence in economics to be appointed in a major university who wished to do research on the economy of modern China and who had the requisite linguistic and historical knowledge to do so. We had even greater difficulty later trying to find a China scholar with the requisite competencies and interest for appointment in the Harvard Law School. But not long after the war had ended, scholars began to be attracted into the East Asian field in increasing numbers—humanists interested primarily in ancient China, but also, especially in the 1960s, growing numbers of others equipped to employ the conceptual tools of the social sciences in investigating the modern as well as the earlier periods.

Harvard was the first university in the United States to offer instruction in Chinese. This it did a hundred years ago in the 1870s, and at the same time it began deliberately to collect library materials for the study of China. Later it also collected, or was given, many important works of Oriental art. But few young scholars entered the field, and for a long time progress was slow. There were occasional course offerings in the history of China and in Eastern art, but it was only after the founding of the Harvard-Yenching Institute in 1928 that more impressive and more consistent study of China began.

The chief original purpose of the Institute, necessarily altered after the Communists took over in 1949, was to advance liberal education, on something like the American model, in China. From the beginning it was felt that this cause could best be served by also developing instruction, research, and publication in China studies, and in studies of those other Eastern cultures which derived from the Chinese, in the United States, in this case more particularly at Harvard. In furtherance of this aim, in the years which followed the Institute brought to Harvard many scholars from the East and many specialists in Oriental studies from other institutions in the United States and from other countries, to the great enrichment of these studies at that institution and more widely in the United States. At the same time it made an additional major contribution to advance these studies by facilitating the exchange of scholarly personnel among countries in East Asia. The Institute also took over responsibility for the acquisition of library materials for the study of East Asia. It has now built the University's earlier acquisition in this field into a library containing more than 400,000 volumes in Chinese, Japanese, Korean, Mongolian, Tibetan, and other East Asian languages which is reputed to be one of, if not the most valuable resource for East Asian studies in the West. It includes in its holdings many items that are rare even in Asia. All along the Institute has advanced studies in its field by sponsoring the publication of dictionaries, language textbooks, and monographs and longer works dealing with the cultures of the region.

While this was going on the University itself took other steps to encourage and respond to the growing interest in East Asian studies. Building on its earlier efforts to provide instruction in Chinese and Japanese (though I have chosen to concentrate attention here on the development of China studies at Harvard, a similar story could be told in regard to Japanese studies), it first established a strong Department of Far Eastern Languages. This has grown into a greatly enlarged Department of East Asian Languages and Civilizations. An advanced program encouraging research in the East Asian field was organized as part of a broad effort in regional studies established at Harvard in 1946, immediately following the war. In 1955 an East Asian Research Center, similar in concept to the Russian Research Center, was set up to further advanced study by various kinds of specialists of both the ancient and modern, the high and the popular cultures of East Asia. Incidentally, the reach of this program has recently been extended—a bit belatedly, it would appear—to include the language, history, and culture of Vietnam. This Center has now published more than 150 volumes seeking to illuminate present problems in the area, always for deeper understanding of the region in the light of its historical past.

By the mid-1960s Harvard had acquired endowed faculty positions in modern Japanese history, the Chinese economy, the Japanese economy, East Asian sociology, East Asian art, and Korean studies and was energetically seeking funding for additional permanent posts in the broad field of East Asian studies. Developments of this kind have greatly increased our knowledge of the East and built up our resources for continuing study of the area, but it would be a serious mistake to assume that Harvard is the only university working in this field. Somewhat similar advances were made at Columbia, the University of California at Berkeley, Michigan, Yale, Princeton, Cornell, Stanford, the University of Washington, and other institutions. There are now perhaps as many as a dozen strong university centers for East Asian studies in the United States, with varying interests and strengths, but each with impressive resources in faculty and bibliographical materials for the work it is doing. And programs, particularly in Chinese and Japanese studies, have sprung up in colleges all across the land, as numerous research positions and many more teaching posts have been created to serve the large and growing interest in the East.

Before the war there were very few American scholars interested in the cultures of East Asia, or, more precisely, very few who were willing to devote the years required to learn the difficult languages essential for their serious investigation. It may be difficult to believe, but our national competence for studying the vast and important part of the globe where these cultures flourish, and for beginning to comprehend the achievements and aspirations of the hundreds of millions of people, strange to us, who live there, was abysmally slight. Now, thanks to many postwar developments of the kind I have been trying to suggest, we are in a greatly improved situation. Today there are more than six hundred highly trained scholars representing a considerable range of interests and skills—historians, economists, natural scientists, students of literature and religion, sociologists, and numerous others—working in the China field alone. The number itself is impressive, but perhaps even more noteworthy is the fact that more than two-thirds of these received their advanced training in the years since the mid-1950s. It can be said that from the point of view of the universities this and the similar increased competences acquired for the study of other formerly largely ignored peoples and places were sought and won for the sake of understanding itself. But it would be bizarre not to recognize that the accomplishment has been, and will continue to be, of incalculable importance for other sectors, public and private, of our national life, for our well-being certainly, but no less perhaps, over time, for our safety.

I have mentioned the Soviet Union and East Asia as examples of areas to which American colleges and universities devoted greatly increased attention in the postwar period, as they turned from their earlier preoccupations with the past and with the West, but they were by no means the only ones. For example, Harvard established a Center for Middle Eastern Studies in 1954 to integrate and reinforce instruction and research in the languages, literatures, history, economics, politics, and cultures of the vast region extending from the Mediterranean to the frontiers of India, a region of frightening economic and political importance for the whole world. Similar centers were established in other universities. Harvard also organized a less formal association for scholars from various disciplines who wished to pursue investigations relating to Latin America, a field in which several other universities made further and faster progress. And as time went on Harvard organized programs for advanced study and research in Inner Asian, Altaic, and African studies and expanded the resources she had available for study of the manifold cultures of India. Similar programs for advanced study of these and other areas were set up in a number of universities to the great and growing increase in our still very imperfect understanding of the many other peoples with whom we inhabit this globe.

As our knowledge of these distant places grew, so in a sense the intellectual life within our colleges, and especially our universities, was virtually transformed. The many interdisciplinary research centers for area studies established in these years contributed a great deal to the change, but it is possible to argue that they were only an evidence, rather than the cause of it, that even without them the development would have occurred. However this may be, one can say that there was no area of instruction at the undergraduate or graduate level, or in professional schools, unaffected by the lively, broadened interest postwar academic communities exhibited in the peoples, cultures, and problems of the whole world. Such departments of instruction as those of history, government, economics, sociology, foreign and comparative languages and literatures, music and the fine arts, which had previously tended to confine their attention to events, peoples, and accomplishments of the Western world, now extended and multiplied their offerings—as for example at Harvard—to include courses dealing with Near and Far Eastern cultures, Islamic civilization, the pre-Buddhist religious traditions of India, China, and Japan and the Buddhist challenge to them. Nor did the newly awakened interest stop here. Rather it went on at Harvard and elsewhere to encompass ancient and contemporary aspects of Africa, Meso-American cultures, the Pacific world, and such other earlier largely ignored places as Soviet Central Asia, the Kazakh steppe, Afghanistan, Tibet, Sinkiang, Mongolia, and Manchuria. The few scattered courses in international trade grew into an extended separate listing of elementary and advanced courses in international economics which were supplemented by numerous additional courses in the economies of individual countries, both industrial and agricultural; the earlier courses comparing Western governments were extended in scope to include accounts of political and governmental developments in Asia, Africa, and Latin America; and the courses in international relations and the formation of public policy grew in number and extended the reach of their concern to encompass the globe. And, while both effecting and growing with such dramatic change, the interests and professional competencies of our academic communities greatly increased in range, sophistication, and power.

Having come this far, I must carry this account a bit farther, for it would be quite incomplete if, having spoken chiefly of developments that occurred within faculties of arts and sciences, I failed to point out that other divisions within the universities were no less affected by our country's new position in the world and the broadened interest in world affairs this evoked. In fact the response made in some graduate professional schools was, if anything, even more marked. I shall endeavor to suggest this, again choosing my examples from the Harvard experience, not because of any special or unique quality it possessed, but simply because I am more familiar with it.

The war had scarcely ended when a Center of International Legal Studies was set up in the Harvard Law School. The motivation for this was recognition that not only was the government of the United States henceforth to be active on the world stage, but that American industry, agriculture, trade, and finance were to be increasingly commingled with similar activities in other countries, and that this situation called for a new kind of lawyer and, therefore, for an enlarged kind of legal education. It also pointed to a need for an extended and different kind of legal research activity.

It was apparently assumed at the outset that this compelling new concern could be provided for in a separate center, but it quickly spread into virtually every area of the school's activity to become an organic part of all of its normal teaching and research programs. The school's curriculum came to include new courses in international law and international organization, foreign law (with special courses dealing with the legal systems of the Soviet Union, China, and Japan), and the comparison of legal systems. Others were added dealing with problems in the conflict of laws which arise in international transactions, aspects of the domestic law of various countries that bear upon international trade, foreign investment, economic development, and the legal problems of multinational corporations. There were still others similarly concerned to further peaceful and productive international relations, including a number dealing with the law of the sea, war, arms control and disarmament, United Nations law, and the protection of human rights.

In the case of this school, as in those of others of its kind elsewhere in the United States, one need only compare the courses offered in 1940 with those being offered today to see how greatly our country's changed position and outlook following the war affected its activity and conception of its task. Legal education is not what it was, nor are the interests and competencies of legal scholars. Both have been broadened, deepened, and enriched to such a degree that it can be said of schools of law, as of schools of arts and sciences, that they were in large measure re-established on new foundations during this period.

Nor were the developments that took place in schools of business any less extensive and influential. Leaders in many countries had been impressed earlier, but especially during the war years, by the economic power of the United States, and this had made them curious about American business management. They were particularly interested to learn how Americans were prepared for careers as managers. Judging by practices in their own countries, they found it hard to believe that universities with their customary orientation toward theoretical studies could make an important contribution in an area inescapably wedded to practical concerns; but when they were told that such attempts were being made in American universities, they repressed their skepticism and asked to be shown. Again I take my example from Harvard, for from the first years following the war able young men intent on making careers in business—at first chiefly from European countries, but later from many others as well—sought admission to the Harvard Graduate School of Business and, being admitted, raised the School's horizons and brought a whole range of new interests and concerns with them.

Case materials were developed dealing with business practices and problems in European and other countries. These had relevance for foreign students, and they proved no less valuable for the American students, many of whom were to make their careers in multinational corporations or in one of the increasing number of

American companies doing business abroad. Soon business executives in several countries, favorably impressed by what they learned of our ways, persuaded officers of the Harvard school to conduct educational programs in business management in their countries, and then a little later asked them to help them set up their own schools of management. Native teachers were recruited and trained at Harvard for this purpose in an International Teachers Program that quickly became a regular feature of the School. The Harvard School helped set up and staff schools of management in Switzerland, the Philippines, Guatemala, and Turkey; at the same time it repeatedly offered programs for senior executives, modeled after its own Advanced Management Program (a program which has proved of great value to American managers and has continued to win their participation and support), in a number of foreign countries. But in this instance, as in that of the Law School, important as were these many activities abroad, they probably contributed less to the new international awareness added to the School's practices and perspective than did the interests and demands brought to the School by American business as it grew in response to the greatly increased range of opportunities and responsibilities opened by the rise of the United States to a position of economic and political leadership in the world.

Let me give one or two more examples from the Harvard experiences to illustrate the point I am trying to make: that the upsurge of interest in international affairs that erupted in America in the wake of the

Second World War effected a virtual transformation in the intellectual range and the practices of the country's colleges and universities, and not least in the aims and activities of its graduate professional schools. To a degree, Harvard's Graduate School of Public Health had always been acustomed to think in world terms. Its programs, concerned with health problems of predominantly rural and economically disadvantaged areas, as well as with those of urban, industrial regions of the world, were unavoidably international in scope. But its involvement with a wider range of countries and its overseas activities increased dramatically in the postwar years, as a steady stream of professionals from abroad, especially from developing countries, came to the School to learn what advances in medical knowledge and medical practice could help them cope with the stupendous health problems they faced at home. Perhaps as many as a third of the students enrolled in this school during this period came from foreign countries. And, while they were coming to Harvard, in a related move members of the faculty of the School traveled continuously to all parts of the world to study and advise on local health problems. They conducted research and carried out experiments and testing programs in the Middle East, in India, in Latin America, and in other places on a number of long troublesome infectious diseases. But they also addressed themselves to such more recently recognized urgent problems as population control, nutrition, environmental health, and the provision of modern health services in poverty-stricken areas of the underdeveloped world. With all this, this faculty's, and the University's, interest in and knowledge of the world and its problems grew, along with their competence to comment constructively upon the latter.

Similarly, the Harvard Divinity School, responding to the zeitgeist of these years, began to pay more attention to the present and to non-Western cultures and raised its gaze to become concerned not only with the ancient, but also with the living, religions of peoples in distant places. In 1958 it set up a Center for World Religions to foster the study of both the historical traditions and the present conditions of the diverse religious communities of mankind. It sought out qualified scholars of the various religions, who were also practicing members of them, and brought them to Cambridge to pursue their studies, and to help interpret these religions for other scholars. This was done in the conviction that such collaborative, committed study could not fail to lead to deeper understanding of the theoretical and practical aspects of the various world religions, and thus to increased appreciation of religion's role in the lives of men. At the same time a somewhat parallel development took place in the Faculty of Arts and Sciences where, as interest in comparative religions broadened, research was increased and more courses were offered not only in Judaic-Christian religion but in the early religions of the ancient Near East, in the religions of Greece and Rome, in the pre-Buddhist religious traditions of India, China, and Japan, in Hinduism, Buddhism, and Islam, and in some African religions.

Having said this much to make the point that graduate professional schools were as profoundly affected by the lively widened interest in international affairs and distant countries that characterized the early postwar years as were faculties of arts and sciences, let me call attention to another aspect of this subject. I refer to the change effected in universities, and in their conception of their proper role, by this new interest. Many universities, especially those of the Land Grant variety, had always recognized an obligation to provide a variety of services as well as to offer instruction and to conduct research; but for the most part these services had been rendered only in the territorial United States. Now practically all universities were drawn into such activities, and in all parts of the world. They entered into contractual agreements with agencies of the federal government—especially perhaps with the Agency for International Development (AID), after its establishment in 1961, but also with other international and private American agencies—to provide technical assistance and perform a wide variety of service functions in distant places which they had never earlier imagined to be of concern to them. University personnel were sent abroad to help developing countries learn to plan and to introduce professional competence into such fields as engineering, agriculture, health, education, industry, and administration in which improvements would have to be made if the countries were to move toward modernization.

I do not know that a full account of this dramatic

rush to be helpful has ever been given. In any case, I cannot attempt it, but perhaps something of its magnitude and extent will be suggested if I mention several of the service activities abroad undertaken at this time by an institution seemingly so exclusively committed to theoretical studies and to basic research as Harvard was, and to a degree would still like to think it is. For if this university, then how much more other major institutions that had long been devoted to applications of knowledge and to service functions!

Harvard's Center for International Affairs, established in 1958, cannot be described properly as a service agency—certainly not as an agency set up to provide services abroad—but it clearly represented movement in that direction. From the first years following the war Harvard had brought talented young careerists active in fields affecting public policy from foreign—chiefly European—countries to the University in summer months for study, discussion, and exchange of information. Issues of the magazine *Confluence* published in connection with this program testify to the kinds of individuals who participated, many of whom have since risen to positions of prominence in their countries, and to the range of their interests. The Center itself, however, was set up with a more precisely focused and more ambitious aim. It was intended to foster interest in international affairs within the University and to encourage research, especially of an interdisciplinary nature, on major contemporary international problems. And these things it did, and does. But the principal reason for its establishment was to provide opportunity for senior officials already actively involved in the foreign affairs of their countries to enjoy a kind of sabbatical in a favorable environment where they could come together with others of their kind from the United States and other countries for comparatively relaxed study, talk, and reflection about foreign-policy issues. The aim was to enable these individuals to enjoy at least a brief period free of urgent and demanding operating responsibilities when they could make use of a university's resources in any way they chose for their own personal and professional growth. The belief was that decisions affecting international affairs that would be influenced later by these individuals would benefit from the increased knowledge, perspective, and mutual understanding gained from such experience. In setting up this center the University's interest was less in the acquisition of knowledge for knowledge's sake than in making a practical contribution to greater international understanding, to improved world order and well-being, and, indirectly, to the maintenance of peace. This is not to say that the presence of these mature individuals, holding responsible positions in the governments of their countries, did not significantly help quicken interest and increase knowledge of other countries, and of international issues, in various parts of the University.

About the same time the Center for International Affairs was established, economists within the University who had become deeply interested in problems of development in underdeveloped countries organized a Development Advisory Service. This agency, which was more service-oriented, sent out teams of economists to work with local officials in such countries as Pakistan, Indonesia, Colombia, and Korea to help them learn how to formulate plans for economic growth and to monitor them. Other teams of scholar-activists from Harvard's School of Public Administration and Division of Engineering and Applied Physics went to distant places to study and devise plans to help governments improve control of rivers and recapture for agriculture lands that had been lost through centuries of salinization. A notable example of this kind of service was a study and report made by one of these teams relating to the Indus River. Even more unusual for an institution such as Harvard was a contract undertaken by its Graduate School of Education to organize and staff a comprehensive high school in Nigeria. I have already described how Harvard's Graduate School of Public Health was active in helping to set up health services abroad, in seeking answers to debilitating local health problems, in working to moderate the rates of increase of populations, and so on in a number of underdeveloped countries. Service was always held to be part of its mission. But I did not mention earlier, as I might have done, that immediately following the war the Law School undertook a program to train Japanese lawyers to cope with the new and unfamiliar complex legal problems occasioned for their country as it was launched on the path to becoming what can now only be called another "Western" nation. This School also instituted, and still conducts, an ambitious International Tax Program, which has now made available through its World Tax Series detailed knowledge of the tax systems of some fifteen countries to serve international business interests. This program has had a special concern to study and report on the effects of taxation on development.

These are only a few of the novel kinds of programs Harvard was drawn into in the postwar years in an attempt shared by many American colleges and universities to put knowledge gained through study and research to work to assist in finding solutions to a wide range of immediately practical problems in the interest of world peace and improved well-being for peoples everywhere. Other universities did more. Through all this, higher education in the United States was brought closer to the contemporary world—to its many cultures, past experiences, and current problems. As a consequence, it grew beyond anything previously approached in understanding of the many countries of the world, developed and underdeveloped, and in ability to teach about them, and occasionally to contribute constructively to their further advance.

If there was one place in a university where the broadened outlook that worked such a radical transformation in its intellectual life was most readily discernible, it was probably in its library. At Harvard this was especially true of that branch of the University Library that serves the Faculty of Arts and Sciences. As I have indicated, a number of the advances that took place in the teaching and research activities in this faculty in response to the new international interest were possible only because of the extensive holdings that had been acquired earlier for the study of a number of foreign countries. Acquisition policy was extended and altered as a consequence of the new developments, with the result that some 65 percent of the materials now being acquired in support of the teaching and research activities of this faculty are in languages other than English.

It is amusing to note that the charter of the United Nations, as originally drawn, made no mention of education. Presumably its framers did not consider education to be of importance for world order or international well-being. But under pressure from numerous more alert advocates the word was added during the meeting in San Francisco in May 1945. The following autumn, at a special meeting in London called for the purpose, the decision was taken to establish the United Nations Educational, Scientific and Cultural organization (UNESCO) to promote education internationally for the sake of improved understanding among nations and peoples and for cooperative effort. The new organization was approved by the United States Government in July 1946, not without controversy. But, though a degree of public misgiving would persist, its goals were accepted as desirable by most Americans and were welcomed enthusiastically by most American colleges and universities which quickly began to vie among themselves to attract foreign students and to establish international educational programs.

It is my opinion, and one of the chief points of this

book, that the increased interest in international studies
of all kinds which followed brought about one of the
most impressive intellectual developments in the entire
history of higher education in the United States. I have
tried in this chapter to suggest the nature and richness
of that development. It cannot be maintained that the
incentive for it originated within the academic world. It
was owed rather to very large forces abroad in the world,
and more particularly to the increased involvement of
the United States in all parts of the globe that came
about following the Second World War. Nor was the
great advance made by higher education in our country
due solely to the efforts of American scholars. American
colleges and universities began to add foreign scholars to
their faculties in significant numbers during the 1930s
as these, mostly unfortunate, individuals were driven
from their native countries by repressive measures occasioned by the political torments of the time. In the postwar years considerably larger numbers of foreign scholars
from more countries were brought to American
campuses. But in this period they came, not to escape
oppression, but because of the more numerous opportunities and the vastly superior working conditions for
advanced scholarship and research available. This situation brought about the much publicized "brain drain"
which saw younger scholars as well as senior ones of high
repute flocking to the United States from all over the
world. They came seeking opportunities to carry on
their studies and investigations in academic communities, but in coming they not only added their talents to

the native supply but also brought with them experiences, interests, and firsthand knowledge of peoples and places, practices and customs, previously only imperfectly known here, to the considerable enrichment and increased sophistication of American academic life.

It was our national policy in the postwar years to endeavor to ensure peace through the creation of a world order built on cooperation in many fields of activity and on enlarged international understanding. The nation's colleges and universities had a role of fundamental importance to play in this, for only they could prepare the highly trained people, specialists and laymen, familiar with the languages and cultures of other nations needed in the public and the private sector, in government and in business, for the implementation of the policy. It is to the glory of these institutions that they quickly responded to the challenge posed by this situation—or perhaps seized the opportunity it presented to them—and willingly and happily set about the task. And the institutions grew and developed in the process, for not only did they produce the people required, and in numerous instances provide additional direct assistance, but in doing so substantially increased their own understanding of the world and its people.

In sum, it seems to me it is not too much to say that in this period American higher education came of age as it acquired the resources, interest, and competence for continued investigation of the needs and aspirations, the cultural experiences, concerns, and beliefs of the whole family of mankind.

2

‣✧‣✧‣✧‣✧‣✧

Graduate Education and
Research Capability

It is a constant vexation to university presidents struggling to find support for their institutions that the general public shows little interest or even awareness of the
upper reaches of higher education. It seems to them that
public discussions of it invariably are concerned almost
exclusively with college or undergraduate education.
They resent this, for important as that level of education admittedly is, they also know how little it would be
worth without the contributions continuously made to
it from academic activity at higher levels. There are of
course many more colleges than universities, and many
more students involved at the undergraduate level. It is
possible to make a case for the greater importance of the
colleges, not only because of the numbers involved or
because their kind of education must precede the other,
but also, many would say, because of its broader aims
and more general purpose, and perhaps because of the
more impressionable age at which it is experienced. I
myself continue to have considerable sympathy with this
point of view.

There can be no question that the undergraduate college was profoundly affected by the great development of American higher education described in this essay. And not only was it affected, but, despite the pronouncements of those critics who could see only decline in all that happened in higher education during these years, in my opinion, when the pluses and minuses are balanced it was importantly strengthened and improved. Nevertheless, it seems to me that the great new distinction achieved by higher education in the United States in this period is owed less to advances made at the college level than to those gained in graduate (including postdoctoral) education, research, and training for research. But to make the point I must go back in time for a moment before dealing directly with the developments on which it rests.

Attainment of the degree of Doctor of Philosophy is recognized as the outward, if not always reliable, indication that an individual has joined the company of scholars. The first American to earn a Ph.D. degree was Edward Everett. At the time a young classical scholar, he later had a distinguished career in both education and political life. Though best known for his oratorical skill (it was he who was chosen to speak before Lincoln at Gettysburg), his career included a brief term as President of Harvard. He gained his advanced degree at the University of Göttingen in 1817. In doing so, he set an example that was soon followed by scores—a bit later, particularly after 1850, by hundreds—of similarly ambitious young Americans. Drawn by reports of an exciting new kind of higher education, a total of ten thousand went abroad, chiefly to Germany, for advanced training before the end of the nineteenth century. The appeal of this education was due to the fact that it was conducted by mature scholars for whom learning involved discovery, and not, as was generally the case at home, by young men of limited experience relying entirely on existing, borrowed knowledge. This kind of learning, totally unknown in the United States at the time, flourished abroad because of official public encouragement and the great new freedom accorded teachers and taught. Those who conducted it were professionals for whom scholarship was a full-time occupation; they were able individuals who were encouraged to continue in their careers because of the high esteem accorded superior intellectual attainments in the adult society beyond the university's walls.

Lifted up by heady education experiences abroad, these young Americans tended to look back in embarrassment, if not with scorn, at the comparatively low level of learning attained in the provincial colleges that had nurtured them. They were especially critical of the American colleges' almost universal educational practice of relying very heavily on rote learning and frequent recitations, in the faith that such procedures would sharpen and fill young minds. But, particularly since they were employed by individuals who had not themselves contributed to advancing knowledge or even thought of this as part of their responsibility, in the view of the young critics such practices were demonstrably ill-suited to fostering powers of perception, imagination, and reason, or to stimulate any eager or enduring love of learning. Contrast all this, they would say, with what goes on abroad where mature scholars speak in learned lectures of their own discoveries and of the great unknown areas awaiting investigation, and where young men sitting at the feet of such titans cannot fail to be inspired to wish to emulate them! They found other grounds for complaint, for some of those who had gone abroad for advanced training came back to criticize the American colleges because of their small interest in science, and others because these colleges seemed inexcusably indifferent to societal needs being engendered in the early stages of the industrial revolution. Whatever their ground of complaint, all of them lamented that American society had failed to provide opportunity for individuals so inclined to pursue scholarship as a life work; they joined in voicing regret that there was as yet no recognized academic profession in this country.

From our vantage point it appears that such complaints were fully justified, in fact that they had been slow in coming, for what passed for higher education in the United States in the early nineteenth century was not very impressive. There was very little support for it, and those engaged in it were accorded slight esteem in comparison with others in business or in the recognized professions of the law, medicine, or parish ministry. College teachers—certainly college presidents—tended to be ministers. The teachers were not infrequently recruited from among those who had not been particularly successful as parish ministers. In any event, there were few permanent appointees, and much of the instruction was necessarily left to young recent graduates who served as tutors without benefit of any advanced training while waiting to be called to a minister's post, or before turning to some other opportunity, usually in either business or the law.

But the young scholars returning were not content merely to criticize. They sought repeatedly from at least as early as the 1820s, and persistently and with increasing force from the 1840s, to correct backward practices at home in the light of what they had learned abroad. What they wanted to do was to turn colleges into universities, or, if this was too much to accomplish all at once, at least to make a larger place in a few of their country's institutions of higher education for mature scholars whose professional concern would be to advance knowledge and to train others to do the same.

George Ticknor, a young professor of modern languages who had been abroad with Everett, tried to institute such change at Harvard as early as the 1820s. But his colleagues did not support his efforts, and, being a man of independent means, in discouragement he soon gave up teaching. Similar efforts were undertaken in other institutions with varying degrees of success; and progress was made, if slowly, in the ensuing decades. Sustained advance began at Harvard in the 1850s, when two distinguished members of the faculty, Benjamin Peirce and Louis Agassiz, who also figured prominently in efforts being made at the time to promote interest in science nationally, took up the cause. Their influence at Harvard was so powerful that by 1862 they managed to secure the election to the presidency of the University of a candidate sympathetic to their views. This gentleman, Thomas Hill, undoubtedly prompted by them, declared almost as soon as he had taken office: "If the genius of our colleges is such that they must be confined to the diffusion of knowledge, and not allowed to contribute to its increase, then it is time we should found a new institution, whose purpose it shall be to further sound learning" (President's Report, 1863–64).

It was clearly the hope of President Hill and his sponsors that Harvard would quickly become this institution, but their efforts to effect the desired transformation met with only limited success. It is now generally held that the turning point in the struggle to make a place in American higher education for advanced scholarship and to turn colleges into universities came with the founding of The Johns Hopkins University in 1876, over a century ago. Establishment of this institution proclaimed that it would no longer be sufficient for higher education simply to pass on what had already been learned, it had also to make a continuous effort to advance knowledge. Thereafter progress was rapid in a number of institutions, until, for example, another professor at Harvard could say to another president in all seriousness (though, happily, many of us who subsequently attended Harvard College would feel, not persuasively) that "the college ought to be suppressed or moved out into the country where it would not interfere with the proper work of the University." (A letter from Professor Edward Channing to President Eliot, quoted by Robert A. McCaughey in "The Transformation of American Academic Life," Volume VIII of *Perspectives in American History*, p. 306.)

By the close of the nineteenth century twenty-five colleges had become universities, and at least a hundred had begun to offer some graduate work. Fourteen universities, self-appointed leaders in the movement to introduce advanced study into higher education in the United States, joined in 1900 to form the Association of American Universities. It was their intention that this association would encourage and guide the further increase of graduate study. By this time the battle was won. College and university teaching had been recognized as a profession, and considerable numbers of able, mature individuals had been drawn into it. Professional societies and learned journals had been established for all the recognized disciplines. And, when measured by the accomplishments of their leading scholars, perhaps as many as a half-dozen American universities had attained standing equal to that of the most celebrated institutions abroad. So substantial had been the advance that, looking back considerably later, President Conant could say of one of the colleges that had transformed itself into a university (Harvard), that "the transformation of a small New England college into a university of national scope and international significance was essentially complete when President Eliot retired" in 1909 (President's Report, 1949).

In the light of what was yet to come this assessment seems to me considerably to overvalue the early achievement, but there can be no disputing the fact that a profound change had been effected in practice and outlook at Harvard, and at a number of other American institutions of higher learning, by the early years of the twentieth century. The critical young scholars who had returned from advanced study abroad set on improving things at home had had their way. Despite continuing complaints and stubborn resistance on the part of less enlightened colleagues, wedded to what they held to be the preferable and more humane values of the earlier collegiate method of learning, there was no turning back. Henceforth the United States was to have both colleges and universities, and differ as they would continue to do in aim, they would live and develop together.

From the outset of the advance just described there was a sharp difference of opinion concerning the purpose of graduate education. Was it created simply to prepare college teachers, or, while doing this, did it not have a more important responsibility to add to knowledge by conducting research and by training successors to carry on this work? It is curious to note that such a famed participant in the movement to transform American colleges into universities as Harvard's President Eliot, who had been trained as a chemist, in the early years of his administration held with those who argued that the purpose of graduate education was to prepare college teachers. He came only slowly and reluctantly to recognize the importance of research as an ingredient in any education that could truly be called higher. The difference of view has persisted, and I suspect will continue to exist and to divide those who are active in higher education. It has led to repeated attempts to establish two doctor's degrees, one for teaching and one for research. None of these has met with any great success, nor do I believe any subsequent attempt is likely to win broad acceptance; for experience seems to indicate that, when two degrees are offered at the same level, one inevitably comes to be looked down upon as inferior and, wherever possible, shunned. This is not to say that there has never been any reason for making such attempts. Despite the emphasis placed on training for research by most of those who have administered doctoral programs, judged by their later performance the majority of those who have won the Ph.D. degree have been much more successful in teaching than in making original contributions to knowledge. Fortunately, many have been able to serve both interests; and, in any event, in contrast to practices followed in some other modern industrial nations, research is almost certain to continue to be a principal activity of universities in the United States.

Noteworthy as was the advance in graduate education just described, there were fewer than 6,000 students enrolled in graduate study in the United States in 1900; approximately 250 doctorates were awarded that year.

Graduate Education and Research Capability

Incidentally, the first earned Ph.D. degree award by an American university was granted by Yale in 1861. Growth in numbers, slow during the remaining decades of the nineteenth century, picked up thereafter, especially following the First World War. By 1940 there were 100,000 students enrolled in graduate schools and 3,000 doctor's degrees were being awarded each year. In addition, programs of advanced study, initially introduced by faculties of arts and sciences, had made their way into a number of professional schools.

Thus, very considerable advances had been achieved in graduate education before the Second World War. Impressive as these were, the quantitative and qualitative developments gained in the upper reaches of higher education in the decades that followed the war greatly surpassed them. This is a major point of my argument.

By 1970 more than 800 institutions were offering programs of advanced study. Some 800,000 students were enrolled in them, and more than 30,000 Ph.D. degrees were being earned each year. In addition, tens of thousands of individuals were involved in some kind of post-doctoral study; and mid-career programs for mature professionals—business executives, journalists, government agents, physicians, health officials, educators, and others—had been established in a number of professional schools. Expenditures for graduate education, and even more for research, had grown to levels that could never have been conceived to be possible in the prewar period. Laboratories, equipment, libraries, museum resources—all the appurtenances of higher education ex-

perienced gargantuan growth between 1945 and 1970. Fields of investigation divided and subdivided; programs of study expanded, multiplied, and were variously enriched; curricula were extended and deepened. In short, during this period the process of transformation, which had had such difficulty getting started some hundred and fifty years earlier, raced ahead, with the result that universities took over the position of leadership in higher education that had been held so long by colleges and became the effective, if not unchallenged, formulators of standards as to what higher education should be.

What brought all this about? No single answer can be given, but it is clear that a considerable part of the explanation for the dramatic increase in graduate education is to be found in the need created by the upsurge in population for many more college teachers. The birth rate in the United states rose very sharply during and immediately following the war years. The effect of this on educational institutions was inevitably felt first at the preschool and elementary school levels. Memory is still fresh as to how communities everywhere hastened to erect new school buildings (many of which, ironically, now have to be closed or put to other uses) and to find additional teachers. In a few years the problem passed on to the secondary schools. Then, as the 1950s wore on, it became necessary to face up to the fact that the colleges were to have their turn, and that to cope with this situation, among other imperatives it would be

necessary to effect a large and quick expansion of graduate education.

The unanticipated population bulge, which occurred contrary to prewar projections, occasioned such widespread concern about educational opportunity that it soon came to be felt that education could no longer be left entirely to the care of local and state governments. Organization of the Department of Health, Education and Welfare (HEW) in 1953, at the very beginning of President Eisenhower's administration, gave national recognition to education at the Cabinet level for the first time. With prompting from Marion Folsom, then Secretary of the Department of Health, Education and Welfare, in late 1955 a White House Conference on Education was called. Though this conference, which was under the chairmanship of Neil McElroy, was primarily concerned with elementary and secondary education, it had significance for all of education, if for no other reason, because it broke new ground by calling for federal aid for the schools and by proposing that the amount of federal aid for the schools be doubled over the ensuing decade. Little federal assistance was forthcoming immediately (primarily because of a long and heated debate over the propriety of the federal government's providing funds for church-related schools); however, a new direction was indicated, and in time advance would be made along it.

Serious attention began to be devoted to the problems that would be brought to the colleges and universities by the enlarged population in the early 1950s. A Council for Financial Aid to Education was organized by five business executives in 1953. Though their concern was initially limited to private higher education their efforts did much to call general attention to the very large sums that would be required to provide the buildings and equipment needed to enable institutions of higher education to cope with the expected large increase in enrollment. The Economic Report of the President made public in January 1954 added the further warning that these institutions had already accumulated a considerable backlog of building shortages. Then, in 1955, a tocsin was sounded that aroused the general public and moved concerned individuals to action in both the public and the private sectors. This alarming report, *The Impending Tidal Wave of Students,* published that year by the American Association of Collegiate Registrars and Admissions Officers, reminded an unobservant public that the war babies would reach college age in the early 1960s, and furnished statistical proof for a prediction that college enrollment would reach the figure of 6.7 million by 1970. Though this figure was considered by many at the time to be much too large, it was in fact surpassed.

In view of the widening concern, it was proposed to call a second White House Conference on Education, this one to be concerned directly with higher education. In the autumn of 1956 a President's Commission on Education Beyond the High School was quickly appointed, under the chairmanship of Devereaux

Josephs.* The Josephs Commission was asked to examine the condition of higher education, alert the public to its needs, provide widespread discussion of its situation, and advise the government and others concerning steps for its improvement. Compelled by a sense of urgency, in November of that year they issued a preliminary report to call attention to the need for greatly expanded educational opportunities at levels beyond the high school, on grounds not only of the larger population but also of the larger proportion of the post-high-school age groups that expected to take advantage of such opportunities. The authors of the report espoused the democratic view that everyone must have an equal chance; but, recognizing the existence of individual differences and interests and concerned about the possible damaging effects of enlarged numbers on academic standards, instead of simply arguing that everyone should go on to college, they made a plea for increasing the kinds of educational opportunity available at the post-high-school level. They were fully aware that the large expansion of educational opportunity called for

* It was a source of gratification to me (and I suspect also, assuredly with more reason, to Mr. Conant) that Folsom, McElroy, and Josephs, as well as others such as Roy Larsen and President Kennedy (whose name will appear later), who played leading roles in the effort to strengthen education during these years, were graduates of Harvard College. Since they also were or had recently been members of one or another of Harvard's governing boards, I should be happy to think that at least a part of their interest in this important national problem may have derived from this experience.

would cost a great deal of money, but being reluctant to advocate any greatly enlarged federal responsibility to meet the need, they recommended instead that each state make a careful study of what would be required to provide for the anticipated increase in enrollment within its boundaries, urged increasing and widening the sources of support for higher education, and said to the federal government at this time only that it should establish a definite policy on aid to education.

The Commission issued a Second Report the following summer, only a few weeks before the Russians launched their first Sputnik. It reiterated what had been said earlier about the difficult situation facing colleges and universities because of the population bulge, then went on to deal with the problem at greater length and to stress the very pressing need for more able, well-qualified college teachers. The Report called for a nationwide effort to recruit talented individuals for college teaching; in addition, perhaps its most timely and important contribution, it argued that if the effort were to succeed, "the absolute highest priority [would have to] be given to raising the salaries of college and university teachers" and urged all who were truly concerned for higher education to work to effect a substantial increase in these salaries. Low to begin with, they had in fact fallen far behind those paid in other professions, which had risen steadily in the postwar years. The Josephs Commission recommended that a determined effort be made to have teachers' salaries doubled over the next five to ten years. (This Report, years before

Affirmative Action, also called for increasing the number of women employed in college and university teaching.)

This Second Report pointed out that twice as many college and university teachers as were then available would soon be needed, and it reminded the public that a minimum of seven years usually was required before a student entering college could be prepared to teach at these higher levels. The Commission urged, therefore, that every effort be made to get on with the task of recruiting and preparing this larger number of teachers with the greatest possible haste. It followed that, if the desired result was to be achieved, universities would quickly have to expand and strengthen their graduate schools, which is precisely what they did. The report also pointed out that if adequate faculty salaries were to be paid and provision made for the greatly increased numbers of students expected at both the undergraduate and graduate levels, very large sums of money would have to be found. It was estimated that expenditures for higher education would have to be trebled, which would require a larger share of the gross national product. But again the Commission shied away from calling for significantly increased federal aid for institutions of higher learning.

Despite its great emphasis on the need for more college and university teachers, the Josephs Commission recognized that it was not this shortage alone that called for expansion of graduate and graduate professional education. No less important was the need for the many other kinds of highly trained individuals required to enable a modern, complicated society such as ours had become to function properly and to grow. Demands for more skilled manpower came from both government and business. These had begun to be heard when it was first suspected that we might be caught up in the Second World War. At that time officers of government turned to the American Council of Learned Societies, the American Council on Education, the National Research Council, and the Social Science Research Council—agencies created by and for scholars in pursuit of peacetime activities—for assistance in identifying and recruiting individuals with advanced training of many kinds who would be needed if the country was to be able to meet its anticipated wartime obligations. Many scholars were subsequently recruited for a great variety of specialized tasks important for the war effort. Most of them appear to have served effectively and to have won respect for their profession. Of considerably greater importance for the large increase in graduate education were the continuing and seemingly insatiable needs of the new industrial, technological, managerial society, which had grown enormously during the war years, for more and more specialists of many kinds.

A preliminary study of the country's needs for highly trained manpower was made early in the postwar period by the Conference Board of Associated Research Councils. This study, made in 1947, pointed to a need for a more exhaustive study, which was then undertaken by Dael Wolfle for the Commission on Human Resources and Advanced Training in 1949. The results of his study (which, incidentally, had strongly influenced the thinking of the members of the Josephs Commission), published in 1954 (New York, Harper) in a book entitled *America's Resources of Specialized Talent,* provided additional incentive for the growth of graduate and graduate professional education.

Wolfle's book demonstrated how essential highly trained human resources were for the advancement of technology, for science and industry, for the military and defense, for health care, for higher standards of living, for dynamic social change, and for a cultivated society. By providing numerous examples to show how specialization inevitably begets more specialization, it made clear that a continuous process was required. It pointed out how developments made in physics during the war years had engendered a whole new world of electronics, and how other discoveries in science and engineering had made possible the phenomenal growth of air travel. It is difficult for us to remember how recently these and other such advances have been made. Wolfle also paid tribute to scholars in the humanities for the invaluable contributions they had made in helping to create the environment of liberty and initiative in which American accomplishment had flourished. He went further to assert that there would now be even greater demand for their kinds of expertise if the country was to acquire the many special competencies it would need for increased activity in all the cultural areas of the world.

The main point of Wolfle's book, repeatedly asserted throughout, was that a modern nation such as the United States had no choice but to find, develop, and use its best brains. He insisted that in making this claim he was not entering a plea for the creation of an intellectual elite, but merely stating a fact. For, he went on to say, "the development of new weapons, the conduct of government and statesmanship, the discovery and development of means to improve health, increase productivity, and add to human welfare, the ability to bring all these forces to the benefit of the less fortunate peoples of the world, and the ability to use them effectively to counteract the influences of totalitarianism, all depend primarily upon those of the nation's workers who labor chiefly with their heads instead of with their hands" (p. 5).

The passage just quoted states quite well a truth that most of us who carried responsibilities for seeking to direct and foster the development of higher education during these years accepted as normative for much of what we felt we had to do. The times called for trained intelligence in ever-increasing amounts. The only institutions capable of helping at this point were the nation's colleges and universities, especially the latter, and in them primarily the graduate and graduate professional schools. We agreed with Wolfle's assertion that "the brains of its citizens constitute a nation's greatest asset," and felt that we were serving our institutions as well as our country by striving to create and maintain nurturing environments for the higher development of those brains.

While graduate education was advancing, and its influence inside and outside academic communities enormously increasing in this period, to a considerable extent it also changed character.

The amount of research carried on in universities before the Second World War was not large nor were many involved in it. At that time the word "research" was heard less frequently and carried less weight in academic discourse than such words as "scholarship" or "learning." Nor had scientists as yet replaced humanists as the most prominent and most honored members of university faculties. Furthermore, there was little financial support for research from either private or public sources. Mr. Conant once told me, for example, that in that period of his many-faceted career when he was a distinguished research chemist, he was considered to be exceptionally fortunate because the Harvard Corporation provided him with a research budget of $5,000, and that this sum, none of which came from the federal government, constituted approximately half of all the support for research enjoyed by Harvard's entire Department of Chemistry. By the 1960s, omitting the large sums paid by the University for the professors' salaries and for other of its regular expenses, this single department would be spending two million dollars annually in research activity.

The vast increase in research activity, particularly research activity in science, that took place in universities during the war years, and continued and expanded in the following decades, worked more effectively perhaps than any other single force to alter the character of American higher education. It has not been widely recognized, but the great development of academic research, which has played such a large part in enabling institutions of higher education to extend their reach and to grow in strength, seems to have followed from a decision recommended to President Roosevelt by Vannevar Bush in June 1940.

Though the United States was not yet officially involved in the war, and majority opinion was still strongly opposed to our ever becoming involved, we were not immune from the shock and dismay occasioned throughout the free world by the fall of France. Some here began to fear that with France fallen and overrun, England would be next, and that then, however determined we remained to avoid involvement, we would find ourselves confronted directly by the Axis terror. Clearly the time had come to begin to prepare for this eventuality. At this moment President Roosevelt turned to Vannevar Bush, then president of the Carnegie Institution of Washington, for advice as to how science in this country could be most effectively organized and used for our defense, and, if it was not already too late (though this was not publicly acknowledged at the time) also to assist the Allies.

After a preliminary conversation, Bush was asked to initiate steps to effect the desired preparation. He quickly organized the National Defense Committee, and, with its support, urged that the government not attempt to build laboratories, assemble talent, and provide the other needed resources on its own, but rather, using the contract mechanism, have the necessary work done by those who were qualified to do it where they were already situated, that is, in the existing nongovernment institutions, including the universities. Being a realist, he also suggested that contracts for the performance of research should be awarded on a competitive basis, the merits of the specific proposals to be evaluated by teams of specialists assembled for the purpose.

Mr. Conant, who was one of the founding members of the National Defense Committee, had this to say of the consequence for universities of the Bush recommendations: "The mode of the committee's operation instigated by the chairman in the summer of 1940 has had a transforming effect on the relation of the universities to the federal government. The pattern set has made the post-war world of American science entirely different from that of the pre-war years. The essence of the revolution was the shift in 1940 from expanding research in government laboratories to private enterprise and the use of federal money to support work in universities and scientific institutes through contractual arrangements" (James B. Conant, *My Several Lives,* Harper and Row, 1970, p. 236) .

The happy results for the war effort of adoption of the Bush policy, and the achievements of American science in and out of university laboratories during the War years, need no recounting here. Dr. Bush played a leading role in organizing research for the war effort as Director of the Office of Scientific Research and Development. Impressed by his contribution, in November 1944, as the end of the war began to come into sight, President Roosevelt again sought his advice. This time the President asked to be told: (1) how, consistent with military security, scientific knowledge gained during the war years could be made public as quickly as possible at war's end; (2) how the war being waged by science against disease could be continued; (3) how the government could most effectively aid research activities by both public and private organizations; and (4) how talent could be discovered and trained to ensure scientific research in the future at the high level attained during the war.

It is likely that President Roosevelt's interest in continuing scientific research in the postwar period originally was due to his concern for national security, for, though he made no mention of the atomic bomb in this, his second request to Dr. Bush, he was fully aware of the importance for modern warfare of the most advanced scientific techniques. But obviously he also had other thoughts in mind. The discovery of penicillin during the war years had demonstrated the value of science for the advancement of health. It is possible that an even weightier consideration with him was a hope that, as science had spawned an enormous industrial development for military purposes during the war years, it might, by inventing new products and creating new industries in the period of demobilization, provide civilian jobs to achieve full employment, as in the event it was to do.

But Dr. Bush's view of the matter went far beyond this, for his reply, made to President Truman in 1945 after President Roosevelt's death, while speaking to the original expectations, looked beyond them to claim for science a broader, breathtaking and enduring purpose. Published under the title *Science: The Endless Frontier* (Washington, Government Printing Office, 1945), it can truly be said to have been an epoch-making report, for it adumbrated a goal and pointed a direction that have guided the development of science ever since.

Dr. Bush's report made a strong case for continuing government support for research and development by calling attention to such recent dramatic achievements of science and technology as the discovery of penicillin, radar, the advances in agriculture that had made possible enormous increases in food supplies, and the new products and industries created through science that had reduced human drudgery, improved living conditions, and provided millions of jobs. It asserted that the national interest required that science be brought from the wings to the center of the stage and be made a proper and lasting concern of government. It added that the federal government would have to accept responsibility for promoting the creation of new scientific knowledge and the development of scientific talent, for only it could provide the large funds needed to further these purposes. Having made these points, Dr. Bush, in sharp contrast to the views of some latter-day spokes-

men, went on to insist—an opinion of crucial consequence for the subsequent development of universities—
on the primary importance of basic research.

He stated that it is basic research, performed as an
intellectual quest without thought of practical ends,
that provides science's capital. He affirmed that what we
had done during the war years was little more than to
apply Yankee ingenuity to exploit basic discoveries
made previously by European scientists, and he argued
that it would be militarily unsafe for us to continue
such dependence. He added that such continued dependence would inevitably slow our industrial progress in
comparison with that of other countries and make us
weak in international trade. And then, the point of
chief importance for us, he said that the most favorable
places for basic research were the colleges, universities,
and certain endowed research institutes, arguing that
since most government-sponsored research would necessarily be mission-oriented, it would always be chiefly
of the applied variety. He spoke of the stronger private
institutions as "the well-springs of knowledge and understanding," adding that they were the only institutions the country possessed that could be looked to to
advance knowledge and to discover and develop the
talent to continue the process in accordance with the
requirements of what he called "the endless frontier."

Dr. Bush's main concern was for science. It was this
that he had been asked to advise on, and he both stressed
its importance for our society and offered a great deal of
advice as to how it should be conducted. For example,

he cautioned against excessive reliance on team efforts, effective as several of these had proved in dramatically successful instances during the war years, maintaining that progress on a board front is more likely to result from the free play of individual intellects investigating subjects of their own choice in a manner dictated solely by curiosity and a desire to explore the unknown. He made a strong statement about the importance of observing academic freedom if science was to continue to progress, and urged the necessity of making more enccouraging financial awards for scientists in the interest of attracting more of the best talents into scientific pursuits. He called for the establishment of a National Scientific Foundation, years before one was in fact set up, and advocated the free international exchange of scientific information. In making these and other suggestions, his intention was to indicate the conditions needed for the further advance of science, and at the same time to arouse public opinion to provide support for the greatly increased and very costly continuous effort he envisaged. In the event his report, which exerted an immediate and a continuing influence on public policy decisions and on university development, served these ends magnificently. At the same time, in it he took special care to make clear that he did not consider the advance of science to be all that was needed for continued national health.

In the section of his report which deals with the problem of the renewal of scientific talent, Dr. Bush entered a strong caveat to the effect that research in the natural sciences and in medicine should not be expanded at the cost of "the social sciences, humanities and other studies so essential to national well-being." But such were the conditions of the time, and so persuasive his appeal for greater attention to science, that many of those devoted to other disciplines would come to feel, not without some justification, that this warning went unheeded.

Whether or not it was done at a cost to progress in other fields of knowledge, science and scientific research prospered enormously and effected significant changes and growth in universities in the years following the war. The Department of Agriculture had supported research in universities at very modest levels from as early as 1887. With this single exception, almost all federally supported scientific research before the Second World War was performed in government laboratories staffed by civil servants. Even so, the total amount spent by the federal government for research and development as recently as 1940 was only $74 million. Suddenly, during the war years, chiefly as a result of expenditures made for research by the Army, the Navy, and the Public Health Service, this figure soared to an annual rate of $1.5 *billion*.

Expenditures by the federal government for research and development declined as the war drew toward its end, and some might have thought they would be virtually terminated when the war ended. But, thanks largely to the kind of thinking that informed Dr. Bush's report, this did not happen. Rather, a new beginning was soon made. Science did become a matter of continuing, major concern to the national government, as Dr. Bush had said it should, and a quarter-century of scientific and technological advance unprecedented in human history was inaugurated. Defense and health being such important issues, the Office of Naval Research and the Public Health Service were authorized to continue to support research in 1946. That same year the Atomic Energy Commission was established to continue and extend the research on nuclear energy which had been carried out during the war years with such awesome consequences. By 1950 the call Dr. Bush had made in 1945 for the creation of an agency to further scientific research led to the founding of the National Science Foundation, organized chiefly to support basic research and to foster education in science and the training of research scientists.

The federal government's interest in science and its readiness to appropriate large sums for its development owed much to its concern for defense. These were repeatedly stimulated in the early postwar years by such occurrences as the outbreak of the Cold War, the Berlin blockade, and the communist coup in Czechoslovakia in 1948, the explosion of an atomic bomb by the Russians in the summer of 1949, and the communist takeover in China that year. It should not seem surprising in retrospect that, faced with this dismaying set of circumstances, President Truman urged American scientists to proceed quickly to develop the hydrogen bomb. But it was not only defense that was of concern to the President and to Congress. There were continuous and growing calls throughout the Truman and Eisenhower administrations for appropriations in support of science and technology in the interests of improved health and medical care and of economic and industrial development at home and abroad. With these, scientific activity increased and prospered inside and outside of universities. Then, when on October 4, 1957, the Russians launched their first Sputnik, consternation struck. Where was our vaunted scientific superiority? How had we fallen behind? It was assumed by many we had. Clearly renewed action was called for, and what would come to be seen as a golden age of American science got under way.

A President's Science Advisory Committee made up of distinguished scientists from various disciplines had been organized by President Eisenhower as early as 1953, but this had been permitted to lapse. It was quickly reconstituted, and an office of Special Assistant to the President for Science and Technology created. The Department of Defense, another innovation of the early Eisenhower years, adopted a new policy calling for the support of basic research.* The National Aeronautics

---

* From the point of view of the universities the role of the Navy, especially in the earlier years of the advance in science being described, was peculiarly beneficial. In general the universities were more involved in basic research than in development, and they were helped and encouraged by the special understanding manifested by such Navy officers as Emanuel Piore and Alan Waterman as to how science works, the importance of basic research, and the most effective role universities might be expected to play in both training and investigation.

and Space Agency was established in October 1958 and, a bit later, an Advanced Research Projects Agency. To bring order into what was becoming a mammoth government undertaking, a Federal Council on Science and Technology, with representatives of policy rank from all the federal agencies that had programs in science, replaced an earlier, less efficient interdepartmental committee.

Science had reached a position of unprecedented public favor. It had come to be looked to not only for safety, health, and prosperity, but by some few perhaps even for salvation. The annual rate at which Congress would appropriate funds for scientific activities began to grow. To top it all, in July 1961 President Kennedy announced a breathtaking national goal to land a man on the moon before the end of the decade; again the appropriations soared. The attempt to place a man on the moon provided a great stimulus to science, even more to technology, and not least to the national economy. But I believe in recommending it the President had an even larger purpose in mind, for I recall his saying to me that he was moved to the decision in considerable degree by concern over the divisions and the debilitating feeling of purposelessness that seemed to him at the time to characterize our society. It was his intent—perhaps guided by some such notion as William James's about the desirability of finding a substitute for war—to arouse the nation to an inspiring task that would cause us to forget our differences, call forth our best efforts, and give us a sense of accomplishment, in the fulfillment of which we could all take great pride. This effort was still going forward when in the early years of the Johnson administration public attention was directed to pressing problems of our cities, and especially of our schools. As a result appropriations for scientific research and development, were again increased, as those made for the Department of Health, Education and Welfare came to rival in magnitude those made for the Department of Defense, and within the Department, those made for the Office of Education those that had been made for many years for the Institutes of Health. It was at this time, before the animosities to be bred among us by the war in Vietnam had really begun, that the great national interest in science reached its peak.

It is difficult to exaggerate the impact made on colleges and universities by the increased attention paid to science during these years. In the early stages of the movement to turn colleges into universities, as stated earlier, in institution after institution the sciences had experienced great difficulty in securing a place for themselves. In this period it seemed to many they threatened to take over these institutions. Certainly they flourished in universities as never before, and in the process the universities were in fact transformed. They became fully committed research, as well as teaching, institutions.

The outward signs of the transformation were seen in the large growth in graduate study and research activity, in the creation of research professorships and innumerable research positions below the professorial level, in the lessening of the amount of time faculty members at all levels were required to spend in teaching in order that they could have more time for research, in the enormous increase in the prestige accorded by the public to research scientists, in the intensity with which academic institutions vied to secure the services of the most famous scientists, in the increased attractiveness the career of the research scientist held for young men and women coming into the world of higher education, in the elaborate buildings constructed in universities to provide for the needs of research scientists, and in the expensive and complicated equipment acquired to furnish them. These were some of the evidences of the radical change, and there were others less readily apparent, such as the enormous advance in sophistication in the methods of investigation and the more rapid rate at which additions to knowledge were made in field after field, the latter with continuous effect on the content of teaching.

What encouraged and sustained this great development—indeed what made it possible—were the very large sums, never before remotely approached in magnitude, that became available for the support of science in these years. The various federal agencies with scientific responsibilities turned to the colleges and universities for assistance in getting their research, especially their basic research, needs met and, even more, for the increasing numbers of highly trained research scientists required to carry on the work of scientific investigation.

They called on universities to manage and staff such large private laboratories as the Naval Biological and the Lawrence Radiation Laboratories at Berkeley, the Jet Propulsion Laboratory at the California Institute of Technology, and the Lincoln Laboratory at the Massachusetts Institute of Technology. Most of these very large and expensive laboratories were organized primarily to perform applied and development work related to defense needs. Nevertheless, although the individuals employed in them were rarely involved in teaching, and their appointments were not subject to review by academic departments, these laboratories provided a great many employment opportunities, and opportunities to continue active in research, for increasingly large numbers of research scientists who were being trained in the universities.

By 1960 the annual rate of federal spending for research and development had reached a level of nearly $8 billion. By 1965 it was $15 billion. If only 10 percent of these enormous sums was spent in universities for research and training for research, even these amounts were huge in comparison with what had been available to them for such activities before the war. I have mentioned the limited budget Mr. Conant had had available for research when he was a research chemist. In view of recent developments it may be even more startling to hear that prior to 1940 all the colleges and universities in the United States together never had more than $27 million available in a single year to support research, and that virtually all of this came from private sources.

By the mid-1960s these institutions were spending at an annual rate of $1.8 billion for research, chiefly for research in the physical and biological sciences, $1.5 billion of which came from agencies of the federal government. It is also instructive to note that the 10 percent of federal appropriations for research and development which was allocated to institutions of higher learning accounted for nearly 50 percent of all federal appropriations for basic research.

In these more recent years three-fourths of all the funds universities have had available to support research and related activities have come from agencies of the federal government. In the cases of some of the most heavily engaged institutions the proportion of their total expense that has come from the federal government has risen as high as from 60 percent to more than 80 percent in greatly enlarged budgets. Since these large funds are usually provided for special purposes, they have inevitably influenced traditional academic practices. Harvard was not among the universities most heavily involved in government research during the war years; yet at war's end it was administering twenty-eight contracts with federal agencies calling for annual expenditures of $4.3 million—almost 21 percent of the University's total expenditures of $21 million. By 1969–70 Harvard was receiving $61 million from federal grants and contracts, a sum that represented roughly 30 percent of the $188 million the University spent that year. Yet, among major universities, Harvard's dependence on such income was and is among the lowest.

The funds appropriated by the Congress for research and development continued to grow, but at a declining rate, until today such contraction has been required as to have engendered widespread concern among those responsible for science's continued advance. But that is not the subject of this book. It is only one among a number of indications that sometime about 1970 the period of rapid university development with which we are concerned came to an end.

The growth of graduate education, along with the concomitant enormous expansion of research activity in universities and the importance and prestige attached to it in these institutions, profoundly altered and advanced the character of higher education in the United States between 1945 and 1970. The changes which occurred were influenced by the altered conditions of life in the complicated, technical society the United States had become and by our country's enlarged responsibility in the world. They were made possible by the comparatively huge sums that became available in this period to support graduate education and research. These sums enabled universities, and in some measure colleges, to increase faculty salaries; to offer attractive scholarships, fellowships, training grants, and other rewards to students and teachers, especially young teachers; to multiply and enlarge programs of study; to build facilities and acquire incredibly more sophisticated and more expensive instruments for research; and so to draw more and more of the nation's talent into advanced study and research activity. They also enabled these institutions to attract large numbers of senior scholars from abroad to augment this country's intellectual resources. Similarly, many younger scholars were attracted by the superior working conditions that could be provided for them here. Of considerable importance in this latter respect was the fact that our universities had broken with the older European tradition in which academic seniority and excessive regard for hierarchical arrangements delayed the development of young scholars. One who has participated in both systems told me that in his opinion a considerable part of the explanation for the great increase in the amount of research that is performed, and the speed with which knowledge has been advanced in the United States in recent years, is owed to this change. However this may be, in this period our universities ceased to look abroad for guidance; at long last they undertook to go their own way with confidence and to lead.

In 1957 a distinguished social scientist, Bernard Berelson, was aided by the Carnegie Corporation to study and report on "what has happened, is happening, will happen, and should happen to today's graduate school and graduate education." His investigation was easily the most careful and most informative study of graduate education in the United States that had been attempted up to that time; his report, published in 1960 under the title *Graduate Education in the United States*

(New York, McGraw-Hill, 1960) , was one of the ablest and most important books dealing with any aspect of higher education written during these years.

The report first reviewed the growth of universities and of advanced study. It then described the current condition of graduate education, citing trends and issues within it, and predicted what might influence its further development to 1976. Along the way the report provided an amusing account of the perdurable issues that have been debated and the recurrent anxieties about trends experienced since its earliest beginnings by those involved in graduate education. Perhaps it is salutary to discover how unoriginal are our best thoughts on the subject. But the main thrust of the report was to direct attention to graduate education, to provide a strong and eloquent defense of the graduate school, and to make a clear statement of the indispensable need of a high degree of specialized study for the accomplishment of its purposes.

Appearing in the early post-Sputnik period, the report had an immediate influence on a waiting public. Recruitment programs for graduate study were stepped up in universities that already offered graduate work, and more and more institutions that had been reluctant to do so rushed to join their ranks. The federal government voted larger and larger amounts in support of graduate study. This led to a substantial increase in the number of graduate students and to vast improvements in the conditions under which they pursued their studies. Never had the academic world commanded more attention or enjoyed greater public favor. At long last the great age of the graduate school had arrived, with the result that more highly trained scholars, working in more areas of learning, were produced by American universities in the decade of the 1960s than in the whole previous history of higher education in this country. Regretted as the achievement was by many, the graduate school had finally and unquestionably supplanted the college as the major institution in higher education in the United States.

Defenders of the college continued to deplore the increased emphasis on graduate education, lamenting the influence the graduate school exerted in strengthening the claims of specialized learning within the college. They also quarreled with the increased emphasis on research in graduate education, considering it a misdirected kind of training for college teaching. And, in the later 1960s, when campus disturbances constituted such a misguided and unnecessary feature of university life, graduate and graduate professional schools were special objects of attack because of their alleged subservience to the hated military-industrial complex, held uncritically by so many to be the source of all of society's ills. But for all these charges and complaints, the achievement cannot with fairness be denied. University faculties in the United States grew enormously in size, in the range and depth of their scholarly interests, and in their specialized competencies, if not necessarily also in wisdom. Specialists of quality were recruited and prepared in far greater numbers in every area of intellectual concern than ever before. Knowledge was advanced. Libraries, laboratories, resources, facilities of all kinds to aid and encourage study and research were acquired and helped to make American universities the world's most interesting and favorable places for the pursuit of learning. And as they developed this attractive, increased capacity, talented individuals came to them in very large numbers from all parts of the globe, enriching them, widening their perspectives, deepening their knowledge and understanding, extending their interests. Universities of exemplary quality had finally been achieved in the United States.

Having said this much in praise of the accomplishment, I must concede that there were and are legitimate grounds for entertaining reservations about it. For not all was gain. The large sums made available that stimulated and nourished the development were not distributed evenly among academic disciplines, nor, it could be argued from various points of view, always wisely or in the best national interest. The physical and biological sciences—the latter especially as they related to health problems—were strongly favored. The gains made by research did frequently entail some cost to teaching. The contention between colleges and graduate schools was considerably heated up because of the large funds made available to support research. At the same time the ancient rivalry among universities for talent, or at least for prominent scholars enjoying great reputations, was enormously intensified. A "star system" developed under which such individuals were increasingly relieved of teaching duties. The wholly desirable advances made at the upper levels of higher education, which should have improved instruction in the colleges, and in many ways did, tended to lessen faculty concern for undergraduate education in the universities. Young scholars were sometimes drawn into fields less because of preference or suitability than because of the availability of research grants or training funds. The rapid but unequal growth of graduate education also heightened personal, departmental, and divisional jealousies and brought rivalries, quarrels, and contentions into academic institutions which adversely affected the even very limited sense of community any of them previously may have enjoyed. More distressing, it became clear before the period ended that the development of graduate education had prompted expectations concerning employment, advancement, and interesting and lucrative academic careers that could not be fulfilled, and so occasioned great personal disappointment. Perhaps the most worrisome and vulnerable development, however, was the greater influence extramural considerations and interests came to have in shaping university aims and practices, for the calls that came to them from outside were necessarily less for the advancement of knowledge than for some kind of service in the light of what was already known. What was wanted in what nonacademics call "the real world" was solutions to pressing practical problems. In the early years of our period assistance was sought chiefly for military and health reasons. These concerns continued, and continued both to make demands on institutions of higher education and to bring large sums to them. Soon there were other requests that dealt more directly with the general economy, and later a mounting variety of additional ones related to newly recognized social, racial, environmental, and urban problems. Practical considerations did to some extent tend to displace theoretical ones, which in the university world probably should have been accorded priority.

Berelson called attention in his book to the conflicts of interest that had already begun to confuse and upset university practice before the great advance of the 1960s had begun: between those, for example, who welcomed the new developments and those who were convinced that increase in service activity would entail a debasement of standards; and—another example—between those whose primary concern was for the college and the teaching of undergraduates, and those on fire to push higher the upper levels of university education, its graduate and postdoctoral activities, and, even more, its involvement in research and in training for research. These and other conflicts were greatly intensified as the 1960s wore on—conflicts between those favoring strictly academic education and those more concerned for applications of knowledge; between colleges and universities, yes, but also between privately and publicly supported—or better, governed—institutions; between leading research universities and those less favored in the amount of federal support they were able to attract; between those in one section of the country and those in another; between the older institutions and younger ones ambitious to develop. And such old traditional differences and quarrels as those between humanists and scientists and between members of faculties and their administrative officers, under necessity usually to make choices among rival goods, continued to flourish and were exacerbated in this period of rapid growth. Meanwhile presidents and deans in universities, forced to live with these and other diverse pressures, took advantage of opportunities as they arose to strengthen one or another area of study or program and then sought additional means to aid important fields and programs of little or no interest to most of the funding powers, public or private.

The great advance in American higher education I have tried to describe in this chapter was admittedly no story of unrelieved success. There were mistakes and shortcomings—perhaps occasional compromises with principle—some of which might have been avoided had the development been managed more effectively. But on the whole, in my opinion there can be no question that it added up to a heroic accomplishment of lasting importance.

On the eve of the outbreak of the Second World War, Isaiah Bowman, President of The Johns Hopkins University, pleaded for increased attention to graduate education. He said, echoing the pioneers who had first sought in the nineteenth century to turn colleges into universities, "Knowledge is not a standardized body of fact and doctrine but an incomplete revelation of the world that is constantly enlarged by new investigation"

("The Graduate School in American Democracy," Bulletin 1939, No. 10, U.S. Office of Education, p. 9).

This faith continued to guide the efforts of the most progressive elements in American higher education in the decades following the war, even while so much of its effort was necessarily devoted to helping the nation to meet urgent, practical needs. And adhering to this faith, in a situation at once challenging and nurturing, the American university grew in strength, in broadened interest, and in increased competence finally to reach the goal that had been dimly apprehended and yearned for by the young scholars who had returned from inspiring academic experiences in Europe more than a hundred years earlier. The higher learning in the United States had come of age. American universities had attained a new eminence. As a consequence, scholarly traffic now moved in the other direction, and many of those seeking access to the higher learning had come to move to, not from, our shores.

3

+O+O+O+O+O+O+O

Finances

Many people tend to dismiss anyone who mentions money in a discussion of education as a philistine. Yet I must run the risk here, for in my opinion none of the achievements won by higher education in the United States during the years 1945–1970 was of greater or more fundamental importance than the success of colleges and universities in securing ever-larger sums to meet relentlessly increasing annual costs of operation and additional huge amounts for capital improvements.

For nine years as President of Lawrence College I and others struggled to make ends meet in a relatively small operating budget and to find funds to construct a few long-needed buildings. When in 1953 I moved to the presidency of Harvard, a university commonly believed to be the wealthiest in the world, I fondly assumed my worries about institutional finances could be put aside. I could not have been more wrong, for Harvard's financial needs were as urgent as those of Lawrence, and vastly larger. Nor did they differ significantly from those of any other institution of higher education, large or small, during these years.

A few figures will make the matter clear. Omitting capital expenditures, the very large sums spent regularly each year in what are called "auxiliary enterprises," as well as a few other budget items usually classified separately, in order to concentrate on the basic category of "educational and general expense," and recognizing that a dollar could buy considerably less in 1970 than in 1945, it remains a startling fact that the amount spent annually by colleges and universities of the United States for operating expenses increased thirty-fold in this twenty-five-year period. The figure rose from a prewar high of only $522 million to $16 billion. It is impossible to understand the development of higher education in the postwar years without taking a closer look at this phenomenon.

There had been very little economic growth in the United States during the decade preceding the war, and many experts—wrong as they not infrequently are—had concluded that national growth was drawing to an end. Then came the war, and as we began to supply tanks, trucks, aircraft, ships, guns, ammunition, foodstuffs, and numerous other goods, first to aid the Allies, but soon also for our own use, the economy took off. Factories were built and productive capacity increased steadily until by 1945, with only 6 percent of the population, the United States had come to possess half of the world's productive capacity. And our economic advance did not stop there. There was a temporary falling-off as the huge war-machine began to be converted in what was expected to be a long period of peace, particularly because conversion was made difficult at the outset by a rash of strikes that broke out as wartime legal and patriotic restraints were relaxed. But this was short-lived. Soon pent-up consumer demands, large programs of foreign assistance, and resumption of heavy expenditures for defense occasioned by the outbreak of the Cold War led to renewed economic activity, and the nation was launched on a prolonged upward spiral of economic growth. The total value of goods and services produced in the United States in 1940 was approximately $100 billion. It rose sharply during the war, and at war's end in 1945 was at a level of $212 billion. By 1970 it had reached a level of nearly $1,000 billion.

A writer for the London *Economist* recently wrote that in the years following 1945 the world saw "the fastest ever growth in real incomes, in life expectancy and perhaps in compassion" (*The Economist*, December 6, 1975, p. 117). Some may question the last claim, but the first two are undoubtedly true. He went on to make the point that economic growth is vital for the function of democracy, and one might add that in this instance it provided conditions in the United States that were extraordinarily favorable for the functioning and development of higher education.

By 1940 our country had acquired some 1,700 colleges and universities with approximately 120,000 teaching faculty, a sufficient number to care for the 1.4 million students, representing 14 percent of the relevant age-group, then in attendance. But the condition of these institutions worsened steadily during the war years. The purchasing power of faculty salaries sank below the levels that had been attained—after generations of effort—in the 1920s. This fact by itself called for a large effort to increase operating revenues. In addition, all of the institutions were faced with huge backlogs of building and maintenance needs that had accumulated during the years of depression and war. Certainly this was true of Harvard. It would have been difficult to meet these needs even under stable conditions—but the institutions were given no such opportunity.

Costs of every kind rose year by year, and those distraught administrative officers who delayed purchasing, or building, in the hope that the inflation would soon abate and prices return to more "normal" levels delayed only to find themselves faced with greater problems. Even more serious was the fact that it was not only backlogs of need that had to be met. On the contrary, the whole enterprise had to be expanded enormously to enable it to cope with the increased flood of undergraduate students, new instructional programs, the unprecedented development of graduate and postdoctoral study, and the vastly enlarged involvement in research. More faculty members had to be found immediately, and even larger numbers recruited and prepared for the future. Many new institutions were founded, while the existing ones struggled to increase their revenues to keep pace with inflation and to acquire additional dormitories, dining halls, classrooms, faculty offices, libraries, laboratories, facilities for recreation, athletics, and health, space for the arts, incredibly expensive instruments for research—these and other things. And no sooner had one lack, or combination of lacks, been made good than others emerged. It may have been a period of relative affluence, but for institutions of higher education funds were always in short supply.

Early in my administration at Harvard, concerned directly for that university's continued financial health and indirectly for all the country's independent cultural institutions that could not expect taxing authorities to provide ever larger appropriations, I assembled a small group of distinguished bankers and other financial experts to help me understand what was going on in the economic realm. I hoped they might give me some reassurance that the seemingly endless wage-price spiral—apparently necessary and of benefit to other segments of society, but potentially ruinous for the institutions of my concern—would someday end, and I asked for specific suggestions as to how in the meantime we might cope with it. No reassurance was provided. It is my recollection, rather, that these experts were agreed that any effective corrective effort would have to come from the political, not the economic sphere, and none of them could see any prospect of such action being taken. They were right. Throughout these years we should have had to run hard just to stand still; but we wished to, and did, advance.

By 1970 there were 2,850 institutions of higher education in the United States, as opposed to 1,700 in 1940.

Not only had more than a thousand new ones been added, but most of the old ones had grown, developed new programs, and acquired new facilities to such a degree as virtually to have been transformed. A combined faculty, not of 120,000, but of more than a half-million was providing instruction, and more advanced instruction, for more than eight and a half million students, that is, for roughly 50 percent of a greatly enlarged age-group, and for a much more diversified student body than colleges and universities had earlier had to cope with. Behind these developments lies a story of great accomplishment, and of very considerable, if by no means final, triumph.

Let me deal first with faculty salaries. To make the subject clear I shall have to go back a bit in time. Higher education provides a good example of what economists call a labor-intensive enterprise, which means only that a very high proportion of its operating costs is attributable to salaries and wages. For most colleges and universities this proportion is considerably in excess of 50 percent. Yet faculty salaries had declined in value and suffered increasingly in comparison with those paid in other occupations during the long years of financial depression. Teaching positions were hard to find during the 1930s, and when found paid very little. In 1940 the salaries paid senior professors in a majority of the institutions fell in the range $2,500 to $4,000. Though the stronger institutions could and did pay higher salaries, the purchasing power of all of them, at whatever level, was less in 1940 than it had been ten years earlier.

It is not surprising that by 1940 a serious defeatist attitude had developed within the teaching profession. The situation worsened during and immediately following the war, for the slight improvements that were made during those years fell short of increases paid to individuals in other kinds of employment, and, more seriously, failed to keep pace with rising costs. The result was that, since salaries and wages were kept at substandard levels in colleges and universities at a time when expendable income available in most families was rapidly increasing, college and university teachers were in fact being made to subsidize the education of the students they taught. They did this for a considerable time before anyone undertook to speak up in their behalf.

Although the American Association of University Professors (AAUP) had been organized to defend and advance the teaching profession, before this time it had paid almost no attention to faculty salaries. It had chosen, rather, to concentrate on issues of academic freedom and on academic and curricular problems confronting college teachers. A few college business officers began to collect and compare figures on enrollment, tuition, and faculty salaries in 1945, but the neglect of college and university faculty began to be repaired only in 1946 when Sumner Slichter forcefully called attention to the financial plight of the academic profession.

He had made a study which showed that, whereas total salary and wage payments in the United States had more than doubled between 1940 and 1946, and family income after taxes had increased by 80 percent, the average increase in faculty salaries had been only about 25 percent, less than the rise in the cost of living. He had also found that increases in tuition charges at colleges and universities fell short of the 80 percent increase in family income, and, however volubly resented, were surprisingly small when compared with the rise in cost of other items in family budgets. He published the results of his study in an article in the *AAUP Bulletin* in 1946, in which, after he had furnished statistical proof to demonstrate how far faculty salaries had fallen behind, he pleaded that an effort be made to restore their purchasing power to the prewar level and concluded by expressing the modest hope this could be done by 1948 (*AAUP Bulletin,* 32:718 ff. [1946]). At the time, apparently, he had little suspicion of how the problem was to grow and endure, but he had called attention to it and soon corrective measures began to be taken.

Perhaps the most important immediate change was the fact that the problem began to be talked about openly—even though as late as December 1947 the Secretary of the AAUP felt it necessary almost to apologize to his membership for beginning to inquire into the salary condition of the profession. The *AAUP Bulletin* had published a summary of a study made by the federal Office of Education reporting the salary scales of

465 institutions, which had presumably caused considerable embarrassment. But from this time on articles dealing with the financial condition of college and university teachers were published regularly in the Association's *Bulletin* and reported widely in the nation's press.

Soon an AAUP Committee on the Economic Condition of the Profession which had long been dormant was reconstituted. The Association began its own series of articles reporting on faculty salaries with an early effort entitled "Instructional Salaries in 42 Selected Colleges and Universities for the year 1948–49" (*AAUP Bulletin,* 34:78 ff. [1948]). After another decade the Association's Committee Z began to publish its regular comprehensive annual reports entitled "The Economic Status of the Profession"; challenged and resented as these often were, they soon became an accepted feature of academic life. These reports provided information each year about faculty salaries and fringe benefits; listed maximum, minimum, and average salaries for various categories of institutions; suggested desirable standards and goals for each type; and graded the institutions on their performance. Two hundred and eighty-two chapters of the AAUP provided the information concerning their institutions for the first of these reports, that for 1958; by 1970 the reports had won such acceptance that the institutions themselves were supplying the information, with 1,367 institutions reporting.

The motivation for the AAUP reports was obviously the belief that publicity concerning faculty salary scales would provide effective leverage for raising them.

Though there is no way of measuring the importance of their contribution to the improved results achieved, certainly they helped. Meanwhile, because of attention directed to the problem by them and in other ways, and through the determined, sustained efforts—more effective than those of the teachers themselves—of administrative officers, trustees, alumni, government officials, business executives, and concerned members of the general public, substantial gains were made, especially from the middle 1950s to the late 1960s, with the result that by the early 1960s the earlier gloom had largely disappeared, and college and university teaching had again become an honored and much sought-after profession.

The figures I set down here to indicate the progress made by 1970 already seem discouragingly small, but in view of the difficulties that had to be overcome along the way, at the time they were immensely gratifying. The average compensation for all college and university teachers, including salary and retirement benefits, had been increased to $14,792 (for the larger institutions this figure was nearer $18,000) ; the average compensation for senior professors had reached the level of $20,398, and for those in the larger institutions $26,880; and maximum salaries, especially for the most sought-after professors, were very much higher. In addition, many professors—particularly some in professional schools of law, business, and medicine—because of the importance of their special competencies in certain aspects of extramural activity, had found ways to supplement their academic incomes, occasionally quite handsomely. Unfortunately such opportunities rarely came to scholars in the humanities.

I have spoken here specifically of faculty salaries, but what has been said of them applies to all other salaries and wages paid in colleges and universities. This, as anyone who has ever worked in an academic institution knows, is as it should be, for the multiform contributions made there by individuals who are not members of faculties are not only essential to the smooth working of the whole, but not infrequently are scarcely less important than those made by the scholars themselves.

The improvements made by the institutions of higher education in their salary and wage scales deserve to be heralded as an accomplishment of primary importance. But this success represented only a partial solution to the huge monetary difficulty with which they constantly had to struggle. For not only did the greatly enlarged numbers of teachers have to be paid more; they also had to have places to live and work, and so too did the additional millions of students who swarmed into their classes. The result was that private and public institutions alike were involved in a continuous search for funds to provide additional buildings and other facilities. Because the public institutions had access to steadily increasing tax revenues, and the private ones were unable and often unwilling to respond as quickly as the growing population required, the giant share of the expansion which followed occurred in the public sector. In 1945–46 the total student enrollment in higher education was divided approximately equally between public and independent institutions, with roughly 800,000 students in each. By 1970 two-thirds of the more than 8 million students enrolled were in public institutions.

On all campuses old buildings were made over and new ones constructed. Wholly new campuses, many of them very elaborate, providing for tens of thousands of students, were built, especially in such large state systems as those of California and New York. This outburst of academic building far exceeded anything experienced previously. With it came many exciting new developments in collegiate architecture. Scores of new, completely modern campuses were established, the creations of a great variety of distinguished contemporary architects; numerous old Gothic and Georgian ones were enlivened by new construction and occasionally completely transformed.

All sorts of buildings were constructed, including dormitories, classrooms, administration buildings, libraries, laboratories, student unions, athletic and recreational facilities, faculty office buildings, specialty buildings for the various disciplines. I cannot begin to give a detailed account of this building boom or describe its more notable architectural and planning achievements, but a few figures will suggest its size. By 1950 institutions of higher education were spending at an annual rate of $1.4 billion for construction. Already $1.13 billion of this amount was being spent by public institutions. By 1965 the rate had reached a level of $5 billion, of which $4.25 billion was being spent by the public institutions. By 1970 the value of the plant facilities available for higher education in the United States had increased from the prewar figure of $2.75 billion to more than $42 billion. The value of all the property owned by the institutions of higher education had grown from $4.5 billion to $62.8 billion (Office of Education Digest of Education Statistics 1974).

The constant search for funds to keep up with ever-mounting operating expenses, which increased at an annual rate of more than 10 percent throughout these years, and for capital purposes, was one of the most conspicuous features of college and university activity in the postwar period of rapid institutional expansion and more or less continuous economic inflation. No institution was spared. Each had to cope with the problem in whatever way it could, and all did, in a variety of methods and with varying degrees of success. Since the general problem was the same, Harvard's experience will serve as well as another's to illustrate the kinds of financial needs with which all were confronted and the immense sums that had to be raised to meet them.

During the twenty-five years under review the annual expense of operating Harvard increased from $21 million to $194 million. The ceiling on its professorial salaries was raised from $12,000 to $33,000. The amount spent for salaries and wages, including retirement benefits, increased from $13,000,000 to $112,000,000. The funds provided to aid students increased from $424,000 to $20,000,000. Its listed assets rose from approximately $187 million to well over a billion dollars. And since

Harvard does not include the value of its extensive plant in its account of its assets, during this period the University raised and spent additional millions of dollars in the renovation of old buildings (of which, not surprisingly, Harvard has a good many) and on the construction of many new ones required by the growth of its educational and research activities. In fact, almost as much new space was added in this period of rapid development as had been acquired in more than three hundred years of the University's history.

Harvard's figures will seem large when compared with those of undergraduate colleges, but by no means so when compared with those of other major universities. The question to be answered is, where had all the money come from?

There is nothing mysterious about educational institutions' sources of income. They are the tuitions and fees collected from students or their parents, appropriations by governments, gifts and grants, and income from endowments. The principal and indispensable source for educational as separated from research and other purposes for all *private* institutions has always been tuition, and so it continued throughout this period. Indeed for most of them it was their very lifeblood. For some it provided 100 percent of their educational income; for many, as much as three-quarters. For only a very few of the better-endowed institutions was this figure as small as one-half. But in these years tuition, by whatever name it was called, came also to be an important source of income for many public institutions. For by 1970, when it was providing 34 percent of the total income of private institutions, it was also providing 13 percent of theirs.

Because of the enlarged population and the greater percentage of the relevant age-group choosing to go on from secondary school to college, after the early 1950s few if any institutions had to worry about having an adequate number of students. It was, rather, the prospective students who had to worry about their chances of gaining admission to an institution of their choice. So, increases in the charges to students could be and were made periodically, in contrast to the practice of earlier years when trustees and officers of academic institutions, competing for students in a market of short supply, sought deliberately to keep tuition rates low. Yet they were never made without anxiety, for there was always the fear, particularly in the private institutions, that the new high rates would make it impossible for some deserving students from families with modest income to attend, despite efforts made to increase available funds for student aid. However, though increases were made every few years, the numbers of students enrolled not only held up, but continued to grow.

Nor were the increases small. The average charge for tuition in fourteen large private universities was only $332 in 1940. By 1970 the average charge in all private universities had risen to $3,129. In all private institutions, large and small, it was $2,719, and in all the public ones, $1,273. The charge for tuition was not the only expense the student had to bear. There were additional charges for room and board and many incidental expenses to be reckoned with. By 1970 the estimated total annual cost of attending Harvard College, which in 1939–40 had been $1,000, had risen to more than $5,000. And the end was not yet. In the most recent statement I have seen, that for 1976–77, this figure is estimated at more than $7,000. Nor is Harvard's the highest.

From the point of view of the students and their families these increases appeared very large; but they had to be made, for the revenues they provided were essential to keep the institutions operating. A recent study of the costs of higher education by the Carnegie Commission on Higher Education, published under the title *Higher Education: Who Pays? Who Benefits? Who Should Pay?* (New York, McGraw-Hill, 1973) , describes what is involved here. By 1970 the cost of operating the nation's colleges and universities, which in the last prewar year had been only $527 million, had grown to nearly $22 billion. Though faculty salaries and retirement benefits, and the wages and benefits paid others in academic communities, had been increased and numerous other improvements and advances had been made, it would be difficult to find evidence of extravagance in any of this. Rather, most if not all the institutions still had legitimate aspirations for considerably more revenue than they were receiving. Lumping the private and public institutions together, the Carnegie study states that in 1939–40 the average monetary outlay by the family per student to meet the costs of education was $508, and in 1969–70, $1,288. But it goes on to show that, whereas the family's contribution fell short of meeting the full costs of the education provided in 1939–40 by $289, by 1969–70 the gap had widened to $2,029. The percentage of the total costs of higher education met by tuition income had declined from 40 percent to less than 30 percent. It could be argued, therefore, that despite the high rates of tuition, higher education was a greater bargain than it had been earlier. The case is strengthened when it is observed that the percentage increase in financial aid for students exceeded that in tuitions charged. In 1939–40 the actual amount was $22.4 million; by 1969–70 it had risen to $2.3 billion.

Though tuition income was a primary source of revenue for the private institutions, more important for the public ones were appropriations received from state governments or, in the case of public community colleges, from local governments. State legislatures customarily vote funds for their educational institutions on the basis of the numbers of students enrolled, and as these numbers increased year by year, so too did the size of the appropriations. In 1939–40 all the state governments together provided only $151 million for their institutions of higher education; by 1969–70 this figure had risen to roughly $7 billion. In 1939–40 state and local governments were meeting a third of the total cost of higher education in the United States; by 1969–70 they were supplying 45 percent of a vastly enlarged sum. Some states, particularly Pennsylvania and New York, were providing considerable support to their private colleges and universities, reasoning that it was more sensible to seek the added educational opportunity needed for their citizens in existing private institutions than to incur the heavy capital expense of constructing more new public ones.

The most dramatic development that occurred in these years in the financial situation of the nation's colleges and universities, private and public alike, was in the proportion of their funds almost all of them, especially the larger ones, came to receive from the federal government. At the beginning of the period the federal government had no intention of contributing to the costs of higher education, nor, despite the early call of the Zook Commission, to be discussed later, was there any considerable expectation or even desire that it should. Citing the fear that federal encroachment could lead to control, in 1952 the Commission on Financing Higher Education spoke out unanimously against direct federal aid to colleges and universities or any expansion of federal scholarship aid to individual students. As late as 1957, in its final report the President's Commission on Education Beyond the High School said it saw no need for a program of federally supported scholarships. Though, as I have shown, various agencies of the federal government spent very large sums in colleges, and especially in the large research universities, for training programs, for scientific and technological research, and occasionally for construction in connection with some special project in furtherance of their missions during the war years, the purpose of the spending was not to assist the institutions, or even to support education, but rather to use the institutions for the attainment of certain pressing national goals. The federal agencies simply bought services which the colleges and universities were better able than others to supply. This continued after the war. The first formal recognition that higher education itself had reason to be considered a national concern was made by President Kennedy in the educational message he sent to Congress in January 1963, and legislation designed to be of direct benefit to higher education came only during the Johnson administration. Meanwhile, nevertheless, indirect though the approaches were, the number of federal dollars finding their way into the operating and capital budgets of the colleges and universities—of which before the war there had been virtually none—had already become so large as to have begun to appear to many to be indispensable.

The so-called G.I. Bill inaugurated the new development. This legislation was intended to compensate and help the young men whose careers had been interrupted by the war, not to aid the colleges. But more than two million individuals attended educational institutions under the provisions of the bill, and in doing so brought a great flow of federal dollars with them. Other federal funds were allocated to provide certain kinds of equipment and to help meet the urgent need for more classrooms and additional housing that had been brought on by the sudden large increase in student population occasioned by the veterans' return. Between 1945 and

1948 the Public Housing Administration spent $160 million rebuilding surplus housing on college campuses, and the Housing Act of 1950 established a program that made long-term, low-interest loans available to build college dormitories, permitting them to be amortized from the revenues received through use of the dormitories. This provision of the act was amended and extended in 1955. By 1965 a total of 2,500 buildings costing $2.8 billion had been funded under it.

The anxieties occasioned by the outbreak of the Cold War led to increased expenditures for defense and the allocation of new large sums to the colleges and universities for research, and for training for research, in chemistry, physics (especially nuclear physics), mathematics, engineering, biology, and the medical sciences. The October 1957 launching of the first Russian Sputnik was an even greater incentive for increased federal expenditures for the sciences, particularly as they related to space. Also by this time awareness was growing of the formidable problem that had been created for the colleges by the postwar population bulge. The conjunction of these latter considerations led to passage of the National Defense Education Act in 1958. Though appearance of the word "education" in the title of this act was probably accepted only because it was preceded by the word "defense," the act did nonetheless provide timely assistance to higher education, especially to graduate education. Fellowships in larger numbers and amounts than had been known were made available for graduate study in various fields considered to be critical for defense, and, to the delight of the humanists, these now included modern foreign languages as well as science and mathematics. By 1968, not counting the many additional ones supported on training grants or research assistantships provided by the National Institutes of Health and of Mental Health, 51,400 graduate students were receiving federal assistance. The amount of this assistance was nearly $450 million. The act also made loans available for undergraduate students and substantially increased appropriations for research activities for purposes of defense and for health. Thus, the role played by federal funds in the operating and to an increasing extent also in the capital budgets of colleges, and especially of universities, continued to grow.

Then came the Johnson years, golden ones for all of education and not least for higher education. The Higher Education Facilities Act, providing matching grants to assist colleges and universities to build some of the classrooms, libraries, and laboratories needed, was passed before the end of 1963—though the appropriations were a bit late in arriving. A Health Professions Educational Act, providing student loans for prospective doctors and other health professionals and matching grants for construction of teaching facilities for physicians, dentists, nurses, and others in the health professions, was passed in the same year. The Economic Opportunity Act, a provision of which made it possible for colleges and universities to establish work-study programs of financial benefit to needy students, was passed in 1964. The National Defense Education Act was regu-

larly renewed and extended during these years, and the
appropriations made to institutions of higher education
under its terms were repeatedly increased. Finally, the
Higher Education Act of 1965 was adopted, the first to
be enacted by the federal government that was concerned directly and unashamedly with higher education.
This act provided for the first time a federal program of
scholarships (as opposed to loans) for needy and highly
capable students. It also doubled the amounts previously authorized to assist colleges and universities to
construct buildings. Furthermore, though there still appeared to be no recognition by the federal government
that the institutions themselves, as well as their students,
needed financial help, the act did include a provision
for assistance to "developing institutions," a euphemism
employed to designate small Negro colleges in the
South. A further provision under which funds were provided to help solve certain urban and suburban problems, chiefly through university extension programs,
seemed to some to indicate that though the federal government was becoming more aware of the importance
and needs of higher education, it would continue to
demand from the institutions aided a quid for every
quo. Yet no less heartening to many than the passage of
the Higher Education Act was the establishment in
1965 of the National Foundation for the Arts and
Humanities to promote creative endeavor, scholarship,
and teaching in the arts and humanities, and so to begin
to do for these fields what the National Science Foundation had been doing for the sciences and mathematics

since 1950. Though the initial appropriations for the new agency were comparatively small, at least a beginning was made toward redressing an imbalance of long standing.

These were perhaps the most important of the legislative acts of benefit, directly and indirectly, to higher education that were adopted during the Johnson administration. There were others, and also many bills, that contributed to swell the flood of federal dollars flowing into the nation's colleges and universities, helping them to survive and to grow. By 1970 some forty agencies of the federal government were collectively spending approximately $4 billion annually in these institutions—or about 16 percent of their total operating income. These federal dollars were not, and could not, have been distributed evenly among the nearly three thousand institutions; for three-quarters of the amounts were spent for research and other services and, to receive full value, had to be spent in the relatively small number of institutions best able to provide the desired services. At best only a quarter of the total sum provided by federal agencies can be said to have contributed basic support for education. Nevertheless, whatever the motive for giving, and however desirable it might have been to have received a larger share of these funds with fewer strings attached, all of them served in one way or another enormously to strengthen and advance American higher education.

Meanwhile, the earlier widespread worry about what might follow from federal involvement in higher education had all but disappeared, to have been replaced, ironically, by a fresh anxiety. For by 1970, as one period ended and a new, less hopeful one began, the institutions of higher education were concerned, not so much because the federal agencies might interfere with their freedom of action, as because the support to which they had long become accustomed for research and for aid to students, especially graduate students, was not keeping pace with rising costs and inflation. It was in fact dwindling, and had in certain instances almost dried up. Furthermore, no new programs of assistance had been, or were likely to be enacted. What was needed, it seemed—what, contrary to the earlier view, had always been needed—was direct financial assistance to the institutions themselves. In the closing years of the 1960s agitation for such assistance became widespread and insistent. By this time The American Council on Education, the Association of American Universities, the National Association of State Universities and Land-Grant Colleges, The American Association of State Colleges and Universities, the Association of American Colleges— these and other educational groups and interested parties, whatever their previous reservations may have been—were all calling loudly for broad-purpose federal grants to be made directly to the institutions. They differed only in regard to the form such assistance should take, for various possibilities were suggested, and each institution, or each kind of institution, was understandably eager to see a formula adopted that would maximize its share. Unfortunately the calls were addressed to a federal government both less able and less willing to respond, and this at a time when families and state and local governments were also beginning to raise questions about higher education and were increasingly hard-pressed for funds.

A third source of income, indispensable for both public and private colleges and universities, is gift income. Though its contribution to operating budgets is comparatively small (a little more than 7½ percent in the prewar period; roughly 5 percent in 1969–70), it is usually of crucial importance, first for balancing budgets and, then, if and when this is achieved, for new ventures and efforts to improve performance. An institution's capital needs (this is especially true of private institutions) are more often than not met from this source. Gifts are made to educational institutions by individual donors, alumni, parents, private welfare foundations, and corporations. Like the sums that come from federal agencies, they are frequently made to support or advance some activity of special interest to the donor; but most institutions accept them only insofar as they advance one or another of its regular programs or make possible a desirable departure in furtherance of its own purposes.

Since private funds were required initially for their establishment and thereafter to enable them to stay alive and to grow, private colleges and universities have necessarily been more active than their public counterparts in seeking gift income. Recently, however, finding it more and more difficult to obtain the tax dollars needed to keep up with rising costs and inflation, the public ones have been endeavoring to catch up. In 1969–70 more than a quarter, $262 million, of the billion dollars received in gifts from private sources by institutions of higher education went to public institutions—and I suspect the percentage has since increased. However this may be, for reasons that have been repeatedly indicated, fundraising for both operating and capital expenditures became, as it had to become, a major and continuing activity for all institutions of higher education, public and private, in these years.

Staffs charged with the responsibility of exploring possibilities for gifts and actively seeking them were sooner or later added to the administrative organizations of virtually every college and university. All sought gifts for annual support, and in time most of them came to undertake ambitious campaigns for capital funds. Harvard's early and successful effort to raise $82.5 million in capital—by far the largest amount ever sought by an educational institution up to that time— simply to meet the accumulated needs of its undergraduate college was only the first of many similar undertakings.* It is a commentary on developments in the period that the goal of this, one of Harvard's earliest campaigns for capital funds, soon came to seem modest, as a number of other large private universities found themselves compelled to seek hundreds of millions of

---

* Large efforts were made later to aid the Schools of Education, Medicine, Law, and Design. An earlier one had been made in behalf of the Divinity School.

dollars in capital funds, and relatively small colleges were appealing for, and receiving, tens of millions in such funds. It is not surprising that during these years fundraising became a recognized professional activity. The number of firms offering financial counseling services multiplied and they all prospered.

Colleges and universities rightfully look first to their alumni for financial assistance; having experienced it, they should be the first to recognize the value of higher education. It is also true that, in all but a very few institutions, whatever they paid in tuition at either the undergraduate or graduate level met only a fraction of the cost of the instruction they received. It therefore seems only fair that as they have been aided by those who preceded them, they in their turn should contribute to ensure that educational opportunities of high quality will continue to be available. Unfortunately not all alumni see the matter in this fashion; but though there is and has been great variety in the loyalty shown to different institutions by their alumni, as measured by either the amounts given or the percentage of givers, in general both of these indices have shown fairly steady improvement. The earliest figures I have been able to find, those for 1952, show that in that year 585,026 alumni of 270 institutions gave approximately $15 million to their annual alumni funds. Not quite 19 percent of the alumni contributed. The size of the average gift was $24.75. When gifts in addition to those made to the alumni funds are considered, it is probable that the alumni of these institutions contributed something like a total of $30 million that year (American Alumni Council Survey of Annual Giving and Alumni Support, 1964–65). By way of comparison, inexact as it is, in 1970 nearly two million alumni of roughly 1,400 institutions gave these institutions a total of $350 million, including approximately $115 million to the regular annual alumni funds. The size of the average gift to the latter had increased to $69 (*Voluntary Support of Education, 1973–74,* p. 10). To give a more specific example of how important alumni giving had become to at least one institution, let me add that by 1970 Harvard was receiving $6 million a year from her graduates through the regular alumni funds (this amount has since grown to $10 million) and other millions for capital purposes. Numerous other public and private institutions, in proportion to the numbers of their alumni, their ability to help, and the size of the institutions' budgets, were doing at least as well.

Individuals are the chief source of gift income to colleges and universities, but there are others. Corporations began to make contributions early in the postwar years, after it had been made clear that they could not be sued by their stockholders for doing so. Not all of them make such contributions, but the practice is spreading and is of considerable and growing significance. For example, in 1970 those corporations whose policies permitted them to do so gave a total of approximately $300 million to American colleges and universities. Of greater importance in these years was the assistance given by private welfare foundations. The

Rockefeller Foundation and Carnegie Corporation had contributed importantly to the development of many areas of higher education from the early years of the century, and they continued to do so in the postwar period, when several more recently established large foundations, as well as a multitude of smaller ones which sprang up in all parts of the country, joined in the good work. Half of the total appropriations by welfare foundations are regularly made to educational institutions. In the postwar period approximately a quarter of the funds received through private gifts by all colleges and universities came from this source. By 1970 private foundations were contributing more than a billion dollars annually to further the development of higher education in the United States and to strengthen its institutions.

I hope it will not be invidious if I make special mention here of the extraordinarily percipient assistance given to higher education by the Ford Foundation, the new giant among its kind, especially from the time it received the vast increase in its resources in the early 1950s until about 1965. For, as one example, it is not too much to say that the very important developments in international and area studies described in an earlier chapter were possible only because of the financial aid and encouragement given by the officers and trustees of this foundation. To their enduring credit and the country's well being, they very early saw how essential it was that such programs be established if the United States was to measure up to its newly acquired, large worldwide responsibilities. Similarly, they were among the first to recognize the coming need for many more college and university teachers, and if they were to be procured, of first improving the financial condition of the teaching profession. Toward this end, in March 1955 the Ford Foundation awarded $50 million to colleges and universities to enable them to increase faculty salaries, and followed this large grant with an additional appropriation of $210 million for the same purpose the next December. In 1957 it awarded a further large sum to the Woodrow Wilson Foundation to enable it to devise and implement a program to encourage superior college graduates to continue in higher education to prepare themselves for careers in college teaching. These were only a few of many unusually helpful grants made by this foundation in support of higher education in the period of its rapid growth and heavy financial need, when many new and exacting demands were being made upon it. The list is long, but it can be said in sum that between 1955 and 1965 the Ford Foundation alone contributed more than a billion dollars to further the advance of higher education in the United States.

It is as difficult to find reliable figures, for purposes of comparison, concerning gift income as concerning any other aspect of the financial circumstances of institutions of higher education. For the most part they simply do not exist. But in this instance some indication of the magnitudes and the trend can be found by making use of figures the John Price Jones Corporation began to collect as early as 1920. In that year they began to keep a record of gifts and bequests to forty-five institutions of higher education; later, when the number of institutions was increased to fifty, the figures were adjusted and the record continued. This shows that between 1920 and 1940 the fifty institutions together received annually an average of $49 million in gifts and bequests. By the 1960s the amount received annually by the fifty institutions had risen to $434 million. They received more than $4 billion in this decade. To be sure, the $4 billion was not divided equally among the institutions; nearly half of the total usually went each year to only seven of the larger private universities. Harvard, perhaps the most fortunate of all universities in this matter, received annually an average of $46 million in gifts and bequests during these years. But figures given in the Carnegie study mentioned above clearly indicate the importance of private giving for all of higher education. For, whereas "philanthropy" contributed approximately $112 million to higher education in 1939–40, by 1969–70 this amount had grown ten-fold to reach a total of roughly $1.5 billion, slightly more than 10 percent of its total income.

The role played by endowment income in meeting the ever-increasing costs of higher education in the postwar years was comparatively slight. For all but a few of the institutions it contributed only relatively negligible amounts, and for many nothing at all. Among those for whom it played an important part, Harvard again must be singled out. In the years before the Second World

War, Harvard derived approximately a third of the income it had to meet educational expenses from its endowment. If one sets aside the large new sums spent on research—practically all of which, as we have seen, came from the federal government—and considers only those items in the operating budget which relate directly to education, it can be argued that this percentage continued remarkably steady throughout the whole period. In this matter Harvard's experience was far from representative. Whereas before the war income from endowments met something like 12 to 13 percent of the combined operating expense of all the nation's colleges and universities, by 1970 this percentage had declined to less than 3 percent. It is of course very difficult to accumulate funds for endowment when an institution is struggling to keep up with constantly rising costs and inflation. But in the changed and adverse circumstances in which educational institutions found themselves in the early 1970s, there was a revival of interest in endowments, renewed understanding of their importance for stability and flexibility, and then widespread and deep regret that more had not been done to build them up in what, looking back, had by contrast come to seem years of affluence.

There can be no doubt that, apart from the disturbances that marred the end of the period, from the financial as well as the educational point of view the years between 1945 and 1970 were extraordinarily favorable for higher education in the United States. Colleges and universities were held in honor and respected for the contributions they could make to economic and social well-being and to personal development. They were looked to for all kinds of services—too many, it was to appear—and they could and did respond constructively and at the same time grew in power to perform more effectively their essential mission of advancing and communicating knowledge. They could do this because of the encouragement and financial help they were given from the several sources enumerated above.

Enormous sums were required to enable them to enlarge and improve the condition of the teaching profession; to construct many buildings and more than double the space they had acquired during their whole previous history in order to care for a rapidly and hugely expanded student population; to make possible and encourage curricular developments and departures; to provide more, and more advanced, graduate education; to gain the more sophisticated and staggeringly more expensive facilities essential for modern scientific research; to fund more and more research activity and support those devoting years of their lives to preparation to carry on this work; and to enable major research libraries to keep pace with the great flood of publications in many languages that poured forth from presses throughout the world. It is a principal contention of this book that the acquisition of the large sums needed for these and other purposes represents both a triumph of the postwar years and an achievement of singular importance in the entire history of higher education in the

United States. Though it was by no means a completed accomplishment, as those who now carry responsibility for the institutions of higher education most poignantly know, it did constitute a major advance both in the resources available for higher education and in the level of academic performance unequaled in any earlier period.

4

Conflicts

Most of what I have said so far shows that the years between 1945 and 1970 constituted a period of unrivaled good fortune for the country's colleges and universities. At a time when the United States had risen to a position of world leadership and, with an expanding population, was experiencing almost continuous economic growth, these institutions were held in high esteem. Ever-increasing numbers of men and women of various ages eagerly sought admission to them, and most of the people on the outside who thought of them thought well of them because of the important contributions they could make to the advanced technological society with global interests America had become. Enjoying great popular favor, they also received far more generous financial support than ever before and carried on their work in the exhilarating confidence that what they were doing was not peripheral to but in the very center of the nation's life.

But there is another side to the story, for during these years some individuals looked upon these institutions with suspicion, if not actual hostility. Extended vituperative attacks were made upon them on at least two occasions—one near the beginning of the period, and another, from a strangely different direction, near its end. Earlier chapters of this book dealt with major positive gains and achievements made by American colleges and universities between 1945 and 1970. This one, by contrast, must describe a kind of negative accomplishment: the ability of the majority of institutions to continue to go about their work amidst the violent disagreements over policy issues, contentions for privilege and power, and various disturbances that marred American society during these years, and to withstand and blunt the threatening obscurantist attacks made upon them.

The first such attack was made from outside the institutions by politically conservative elements in the population who considered that the colleges and universities had been taken over by individuals holding excessively liberal, if not downright radical, views. In their opinion these institutions were working to subvert the society that had created them. There had been an earlier fear of communism in the 1930s. Though most of those suspected of treasonable communist sympathies at that time were associated in one way or another with the labor movement, many of the conservative opponents of President Roosevelt's New Deal had also looked upon professors with suspicion, believing that they deceitfully taught ideas subversive of American values and therefore constituted a danger to the republic. When the House Un-American Activities Committee was established in 1934, the majority of Americans probably thought that the more serious threat to democracy lay on the right. This group, with a largely conservative membership, descried it on the left and very quickly numbered academics among those they considered especially untrustworthy.

The fear of communism tended to subside during the war years, when we were allied with the Russians, but it revived with the outbreak of the Cold War, and this time professors were in the direct line of fire. A charge of treason was raised early in 1945, before the war had ended, when it was disclosed that confidential documents, including some marked top secret, had been made available to the editors of the magazine *Amerasia*. Though no indictments were made at that time, concern increased rapidly thereafter, as Russia began to extend her power and influence in Eastern Europe and communism began to advance in East Asia. In March 1946, speaking in Fulton, Missouri, Churchill warned that "an iron curtain had descended across the continent of Europe." His speech occasioned no great excitement, but suspicion of Russia's intentions and fears concerning our own internal security were substantially intensified later that year when the effective wartime activity of a spy ring in Canada was disclosed and it also became unmistakably clear that espionage had been going on in the United States for some time. Worries mounted and soon took on political significance. A comprehensive loyalty check of all federal employees was instituted in 1947, and in March of that year the

Truman Doctrine, calling for economic and military aid by the United States for any nation threatened by communism and support for free people everywhere who resisted subjugation, was adopted. The following summer a National Security Act was passed. In June 1948 the Berlin Blockade (which was to last more than a year) began, and a peacetime Selective Service program was instituted. Anxiety about Russia's intentions, and even more about internal security, continued to grow; it increased startlingly when in August 1948 Whittaker Chambers renewed his charges, earlier ignored, that Alger Hiss had repeatedly betrayed secrets to the Russians while in the employ of the government during the 1930s.

Americans found these developments disturbing; and there were more to come. In 1949 China was taken over by communists, Judith Coplon was picked up as a spy in the United Nations, and President Truman announced that the Russians had exploded an atomic bomb. It is not surprising that in that year the several military services were united in the newly formed Department of Defense, the North Atlantic Treaty Organization (NATO) was established, and the leaders of the American Communist Party were convicted on charges of conspiracy to advocate the violent overthrow of the United States Government. To cap all these incitements to anxiety and fear, in January 1950 Alger Hiss was convicted of perjury, with the clear implication that he had indeed been cooperating with communists serving Russia. This was followed early the next month by the devastating revelation that the German refugee physicist Klaus Emil Fuchs, who had played a prominent role at Los Alamos in the development of the atomic bomb, and who had just been arrested by the British, had all along been a Russian agent. At this point the renewed anti-communist fear, which had been growing from at least early 1945, broke into flame.

Disturbed by all these developments, Americans became frightened, anxious, and bewildered. Most liberals and intellectuals tended to discount the various disclosures and charges, dismissing them—and many, though by no means all, of them were—as hallucinations or fabrications by right-wing reactionaries. But their sometimes hysterical rejoinders brought little reassurance to those who were not already of their persuasion, and the unease mounted. The notion of a vast and powerful communist conspiracy to subvert the United States gained credibility and for a time, aided by the accusations of a growing number of anti-communist vigilantes, began to feed on itself. Charges, allegations, and insinuations of disloyalty, originally made against a number of people in government service, were next leveled against many individuals of known liberal sympathies employed in the communications and entertainment industries, and then again, as in the 1930s and this time with special vehemence, against academics.

In the late 1940s, especially after Congressman Harold Velde of Illinois, who proclaimed that Soviet spies were infesting the entire country, became its chairman, the House Un-American Activities Committee renewed its efforts to ferret out subversives in academic communities; and the Senate's Internal Security sub-committee, under the leadership of another anti-communist vigilante, William Jenner of Indiana, was no less energetic in the search. To their relentless efforts (many would say, to their abusive tactics) there were added, early in 1950, those of Senator Joseph McCarthy of Wisconsin. This opportunist, who perceived in a situation already heated up an opportunity for self aggrandizement, seized leadership of the anti-communist crusade and cynically began to make reckless inflammatory accusations, wild threats, and charges, many directed against individuals in colleges and universities. He continued to do so without interruption until the Senate finally summoned sufficient courage to pass a vote of censure against him in December 1954.

These were trying times for members of faculties, especially for those who attracted the attention of any of the investigating agencies, and no less so for administrative officers and trustees charged with the public defense of their institutions. Their task was made difficult by the fact that there were communists and communist sympathizers in the United States, in and out of the colleges and universities, and it was commonly held that members of the party were under obligation to follow policies dictated from abroad. There had been some communists in the nation's colleges in the 1930s, and, harder to explain, some were still present in the later 1940s. But their numbers were never large, nor did their influence have anything like the potential that was alleged and feared.

Members of my generation will recall that there was considerable criticism of American society as early as the 1920s, when many had already come to feel that Western capitalistic society was limited and dehumanizing because of its headlong pursuit of materialistic ends and its indifference to concerns of beauty. This criticism continued and increased in the 1930s when the fault-finding shifted to social and economic grounds, and many began to see special merit in Russia. The most perceptive account I know of the intellectual climate of these years in which individuals were attracted to communism is that given in the novel Lionel Trilling published in 1948, *The Middle of the Journey* (New York, Viking). In it he described how certain idealists, and others inclined for a variety of reasons to disparage American society, began to proclaim that a society founded on reason and virtue could be achieved, that Russia provided the model for it, and that it was on its way to becoming a reality even here.

It is not difficult to see the appeal such a vision might have for the inexperienced, optimistic, and well-meaning, or the opportunity the disaffected and designing would certainly see in it. A number of Americans, including some college and university teachers, most of them kindly disposed toward their fellowmen, did find their way into the Communist Party, and a considerably larger number came to express sympathy with causes the party espoused. *Scoundrel Time* (Boston, Little, Brown, 1976), Lillian Hellman's recent book, indirectly confirms the fascination communism, Russia, and an assortment of ideas critical of the United States had for "liberals" in the 1930s and 1940s and helps to explain how so many, from idealistic motives and wishful thinking, could become fellow travelers. It is considerably more difficult to understand the slowness with which some of those who had been beguiled by the enchanting vision came to recognize and admit that it did not exactly square with reality. But in my opinion very few academics were in any sense involved in a conspiracy; and very little, if any, either of what the majority of them believed, or of what they did, warranted the vicious, false, and demeaning charges that were often leveled against them—and by extension against the whole academic profession—in the late 1940s and early 1950s by self-appointed protectors of the American way.

These zealots, usually referring to academics sneeringly as "perfessors," found them easy targets in their vituperative rhetoric, making them scapegoats for all the shortcomings, failures, and frustrations of American society. More serious was the fact that their charges were reinforced and magnified by constant repetition in the media, and so contagious was the disease thus planted in the minds of otherwise fairly reasonable people, including members of boards of trustees, and so powerful to feed fears and stimulate tormented imaginings that many came to believe there must be justification for the attacks. At the next stage the less scrupulous among them joined the attack; and so their numbers grew, until by 1949 state legislatures in all parts of the country, urged on by American Legionnaires, frightened parents, and many other narrowly patriotic citizen groups, undertook to censor textbooks and curricula in schools and colleges and, where they did not already exist, to pass laws requiring loyalty oaths of all teachers—of teachers as a special class.

An early instance of this sort of thing which attracted widespread attention in academic circles took place at the University of California in Berkeley. Here the University's Board of Regents added to the oath of loyalty to the state and federal constitutions, already mandatory for all state employees, a requirement that every member of the University faculty also swear that he was not a member of the Communist Party or under any obligation that would in any way conflict with his oath of loyalty. One could find fault with the requirement on the ground that at that time the Communist Party was still a legal party in the state; a much more serious concern for faculty members was the conviction many of them held that the oath constituted an infringement of academic freedom because it implied that in certain areas of academic study a professor was not to be permitted to arrive at opinions solely on the basis of his research. Perhaps even more distasteful was the fact that the legislation seemed to require professors to swear not only that they were not communists, but that they were not lying when they swore.

A brouhaha immediately broke out which academics

everywhere followed with intense interest. Not all of the Regents had approved of the requirement when it was first enacted, and later a modification was worked out which enabled most of the faculty to sign in good conscience. But thirty-nine who continued to refuse were dismissed. They pursued the matter in the courts, where in time the supreme court of the state ruled against the requirement, stating that since the matter with which it was concerned was adequately taken care of by the loyalty oath itself, there was no need to add a clause addressed specifically to professors. But it is doubtful that this solution was fully satisfactory either to the harried professors or to those suspicious of them, intent on rooting out the communists they confidently believed were to be found in their ranks.

The search for communist professors continued for a number of years on campuses throughout the United States. The various investigating bodies subpoenaed individuals suspected of membership in the Communist Party and insisted that they declare if they were or ever had been members of that party. Many refused to reply, citing the Fifth Amendment in their defense, but in the mood of the time such action tended only to confirm the original suspicion. It *was* a "scoundrel time"; but the issue raised was and remains a difficult one, and only those unable to see its complexities, or with a cause to advance, insisted then, and insist now, that there was a single, correct way of dealing with the cases that arose. Many who were not zealots agreed that membership in the Communist Party was a clear indication that a person was unfitted for a teaching position, since it was generally believed that members of the party, being under discipline, were required to follow the party line, and so not only were not free to pursue the truth if it led in an unapproved direction, but were committed to inexcusable policies of secrecy and dissembling. And it was accepted by almost all academics that their job was to seek the truth and not to try directly to make over society. The cautionary statement made by the members of the Harvard Corporation at the time, in recording action they had taken in several cases of alleged communist membership with which they had to deal, and in which they stated that absent some very exceptional circumstances they would not knowingly appoint a communist to the faculty, reflected these beliefs.

With all the searching, very few proven communists were discovered in faculty ranks. Nevertheless, it was an agitated and difficult time for members of faculties, and, as I have said, no less so for administrative officers and trustees. The latter, sensitive to the importance and requirements of academic freedom, were frequently called upon to defend publicly individuals who were not the most convincing representatives of their profession, in cases where it was often virtually impossible to defend scholarly independence without at the same time protecting unattractive extracurricular or extramural activities that were quite unrelated to scholarly concerns.

Admittedly, not all responsible groups stood firm against the storm (we have already seen that some of the Regents of the University of California failed to do so) ;

but a sufficient number did to ensure the vitality of higher education in the United States and to enable it to continue to grow. The more courageous among them—or perhaps only the better informed, or more clear-sighted—did not succumb to the fear of subversion rampant at the time. Instead, they recognized that the number and influence of the subversives were grossly exaggerated, and then in sober mood challenged the claim of the many zealots who, while professing to protect the American way, would in fact have destroyed it by restricting the free expression of opinion in a misguided effort to enforce a narrow national conformity.

But as attacks on colleges and universities had not begun with Senator McCarthy, so they did not end with his censure by the Senate. Suspicion of intellectuals, and so of academics, goes far back and lies deep in American society. It may well have been present in some degree from our country's beginning. However this may be, in recent times, for one reason or another, the nation's institutions of higher education have been hampered by a continuous crossfire between liberal and conservative elements in our population. The passage of the National Defense Education Act in 1958 occasioned a fresh outbreak of an old trouble.

As was mentioned earlier, this act was of epoch-making importance and brought great benefit to higher education; but when it was enacted it also gave extreme conservatives in the Congress a fresh opportunity to show their distrust of and animosity toward academics, by imposing upon them another requirement of a spe-

cial oath and a disclaimer affidavit. Though this oath
and the disclaimer affidavit had appeared in exactly the
same words in the National Science Foundation Act of
1950, they did not provoke active opposition at that
time, presumably because under the provisions of that
act the students involved were expected to deal directly
and independently with the government, and the institutions apparently felt that it was improper for them to
tell the students what to do. I cannot be certain of this,
for I was not in the university world at the time. But
there can be no mistaking the fact that under the terms
of the National Defense Education Act educational institutions were put in the position of being partners
with the government, required to exact oaths and disclaimer affidavits from students in exchange for grants
and loans. This was a different matter. Furthermore,
since a portion of the funds had to be supplied by the
institutions themselves, it appeared that the government
was beginning to regulate the institutions' use of their
own resources. Concerned about these implications in
the legislation, a number of individuals within the
academic community—of whom this time I was one—
undertook to try to have the oath-affidavit requirement
repealed. After several years, through the efforts of
many, we finally succeeded in having the requirement
of the disclaimer affidavit eliminated, but not that of the
loyalty oath.

The article to which we objected stated that anyone
who received funds under the provisions of the act
should swear an oath of allegiance to the United States

and of readiness to defend its Constitution and laws and, in addition, should swear a disclaimer affidavit "that he does not believe in, and is not a member of and does not support any organization that believes in or teaches, the overthrow of the United States Government by force or violence or by any illegal or unconstitutional methods."

It is an interesting indication of a persistent division within American society—and of the continued presence among us of a good many superpatriots, convinced of the existence of a widespread conspiracy to overthrow the United States Government—that the John Birch Society was founded in the same year the National Defense Education Act was passed. Its members and others who held similar views were certain such a conspiracy existed and that its advance was aided by the misguided complacency of many fellow travelers, whose more influential echelons were made up largely of college and university professors. Individuals of their persuasion could quite honestly see no reason why any loyal American would hesitate—indeed would not welcome the opportunity—to swear the kind of extended oath required by the act. But there were, and are, very good reasons.

In the first place, the requirement was resented by many in the academic world as an unjustified and unwarranted affront, since it singled out members of their profession from among all groups in the nation for special distrust. In addition, such a requirement seemed to them futile, for they believed, probably correctly, that anyone seriously set on overthrow of the government would not hesitate to swear this or any other oath if asked to do so. A more serious consideration was that the requirement appeared to them an attempt to impose thought control, and, as such, was an intolerable violation of one of the fundamental principles of our society. They pointed out that it was a cardinal belief of the founding fathers that individuals should never be punished for beliefs entertained, but only for illegal acts committed, and that this continued to constitute an essential element in the preservation of personal liberty.

We outraged academics therefore held, in contradistinction to those who sought to impose the test oath, that in the United States it was the essence of patriotism to stand for freedom of conscience and belief, rights guaranteed to every citizen by the First Amendment, and that since this was so we would not, nor should any loyal American, ever swear such an oath as the disclaimer affidavit, which threatened individuals with disabilities not because of any illegal act, but because of beliefs. It did not follow that we endorsed the beliefs our opponents were worried about. Furthermore, being familiar with youthful idealism, we felt reasonably sure that those most likely to be hurt by refusing to take the oath would almost certainly be young men and women of high principle, possibly among the best of their generation, the very kind of superior individuals whose development other provisions in the act were designed to assist in the interest of increased national security. It seemed to us sadly mistaken to imagine that security could be attained through restrictive legislation.

It was a very difficult matter during all these years for

those who guided, or attempted to guide, institutions of
higher education to find a defensible course amidst the
conflicts of liberals and conservatives, both eager and
striving to use these institutions for their own partisan
purposes. To go back no further, combativeness between "left-wingers" and "right-wingers" was a marked
characteristic of the period of President Roosevelt's New
Deal, as all who were alive at the time will remember.
Though this quarrel was muted during the war years, it
was by no means ended. The contest was between those
who looked to the federal government for amelioration
of social and economic ills and those who considered any
movement in this direction to be without promise, if
not actually dangerous to national health and subversive
of individual liberty.

The federal government was under more or less constant attack during the Roosevelt years by members of
the business community, the National Association of
Manufacturers, the Chamber of Commerce, the American Legion, the American Liberty League, and a
plethora of other conservatives and conservative organizations. On the other hand, the administration had its
liberal defenders, who surely must have outnumbered
the attackers, since it was repeatedly continued in
power. Among the most convinced and articulate of the
latter were many from the ranks of college and university faculties. Though the sharp and often very bitter
difference of opinion on economic, social, and political
issues existed within academic communities in roughly
the same proportions as outside, the prominence of sev-

eral of these liberal faculty spokesmen led conservative elements outside—especially the more extreme among them who were not given to making nice distinctions— to identify academic communities wholesale with the left. As a result, these institutions incurred their anger, hostility, and lasting distrust.

Active strife, renewed between the partisans when the war ended, continued throughout the whole period under review. Those of the liberal persuasion were eager to continue and advance the social reforms that had been begun under the New Deal: to increase educational and economic opportunity, to provide for welfare and medical care, and to move further along the road toward the achievement of equality in all areas. Their opponents, though not necessarily disagreeing about the ends sought, strenuously objected to the increasing assumption of power by the federal government and the growth of the federal bureaucracy and called for restraint in spending and for limited government. Though differences of opinion existed within both major political parties—and indeed within and among all other identifiable groups in the American population—by and large liberals, always seeking to advance social welfare reforms, tended to identify with the Democratic party, while their conservative counterparts, striving just as assiduously to slow down if not actually to prevent such action, were more likely to be found in the Republican camp.

President Truman was the leader of the liberal faction in the immediate postwar period, Senator Taft of the opposition. Senator Taft not only opposed President Truman's Fair Deal program (most of which the Republicans succeeded in defeating with the aid of Southern Democrats) but also quarreled with his foreign policies. Apparently failing to understand the change that had occurred in the American public concerning our country's participation in international affairs and so overestimating the hold of the old isolationism on the popular mind, in 1951, in an effort to win the Republican nomination for the presidency, he opened what he called a "Great Debate" on foreign policy. But he lost the nomination to the moderate Republican, Dwight D. Eisenhower, who was committed to international policies, and who before the end of his administration was to succeed in making our participation in the United Nations acceptable to the great majority of Republicans.

Eisenhower won election over the more liberal Democratic candidate, Adlai Stevenson, who had wide and enthusiastic support in the academic world, in 1952, and again in 1956, the latter time by a landslide. The years of his administration have in later years often been referred to as a do-nothing period, but at least from the point of view of institutions of higher education this seems to me demonstrably unfair. Following the conclusion of the Korean War, they constituted a prolonged, relatively calm, and constructive period favorable both for academic institutions and for the country at large. The private and the public sectors worked fairly harmoniously together in a time of peace and steady economic growth. It was a period of impressive technological and industrial advance that had the effect of making life easier and more enjoyable for many people, one in which extremists on both flanks of the political spectrum were comparatively subdued. People "liked Ike" at home and abroad, and in the calm, if that is what it is to be called, much was done to strengthen higher education.

Two White House Conferences on education were held. The Department of Health, Education and Welfare was organized. Considerable attention was devoted to means of widening educational opportunity. The battle to end segregation in education on racial grounds was begun. The Civil Rights Commission was established. Successful efforts to improve faculty salaries were encouraged. Important measures were taken to strengthen graduate education and to augment the national capability in science and in international activity. A federal program providing medical care for the aged and the needy was enacted, and steps were taken to advance medical education and medical research. Cultural exchanges were begun with the Soviet Union. Other advances with broad economic impact—such as the Housing Act, passed early in the administration, which enabled many people to acquire homes, the Federal Highway Program, and an exceptionally constructive Agricultural Act—were indirectly helpful to institutions of higher education. Finally, in 1958 the National Defense Education Act was passed; despite the imperfection in it, discussed above, it marked the beginning of the very great development in institutions of higher education that took place in the following two Democratic administrations.

But, as has already been demonstrated, the early to middle 1960s were the golden age for higher education. Yet, even in this happy period the quarrels between liberals and conservatives, especially between the more extreme elements in both camps, over issues of public policy and the requirements of national security, which continuously threatened to impede the advance of the institutions of higher education, did not entirely disappear. The tides of public opinion moved back and forth between liberal and conservative points of view, between efforts to advance social programs through the agency of the federal government and efforts to hold them back. There was never a time free of heated public controversy, as the juxtaposed names of Nelson Rockefeller and Richard Nixon, Nixon and John Kennedy, Lyndon Johnson and Barry Goldwater, and Hubert Humphrey and again Nixon will serve to recall.

In all of these contests members of faculties, and occasionally the chief administrative officers of some of the institutions of higher education, publicly espoused one position or another and joined in debate in an effort to influence public opinion. Some, untroubled by any doubt concerning the correctness and universal validity of their opinions, maintained that such activity was a social obligation, even a moral responsibility of academics (their numbers were to grow as the years wore on). The great majority of those in academic life, however, continued to believe, at least into the latter years of the 1960s, that they had important work of a special kind which it was their responsibility—and an absorbing task—to perform and that they could do this best if they as academics, and their institutions as institutions, adhered to a policy of standing apart from political controversies which did not directly threaten to impair their ability to do this work.

Alas, this was soon to change! In a few short years this earlier hard-won view of the academic's responsibility came to many to seem at best naive and, far more often, deliberately hypocritical. The stages by which the new view came to win acceptance constitute a story in themselves.

The line of development that was to cause many students and faculty members to turn against the policy of detachment began to show itself at least as early as the middle 1950s, when the wide publicity given the successful boycott by blacks of the public buses in Montgomery, Alabama, in 1956, over the issue of segregation, stirred the consciences of many Americans, including many in the academic world. This incident greatly increased sensitivity to the injustices which had long habitually been visited on black citizens and had the additional effect of catapulting its leader, the youthful Martin Luther King, into national prominence. Four years later, when four black students of the North Carolina Agricultural and Technical College summoned up the courage to sit down at a segregated white lunch counter in a Woolworth store in Greensboro, white students from many campuses, joined by faculty members and others, sought to aid them by staging demonstrations in many places throughout the country. Soon thereafter sit-ins and demonstrations—nonviolent ones in the early years—became a way of life for many Americans, young and old, from inside and outside academic communities. Conducted with increasing frequency, and with mounting disturbance of traditionally sheltered scholarly pursuits, such tactics were used effectively to end segregation in interstate travel, to gain admission for black students to segregated colleges and universities in the South, to register black voters, to gain equal treatment for blacks under the law, and in general to put an end to all "separate but equal" practices.

During the early 1960s many people, including large contingents from academic communities, became outraged at the long-standing mistreatment of blacks and eagerly joined in a whole range of activities in a determined effort to eradicate all traces of racial discrimination from American life. At the time they were confident this could be done easily and quickly by peaceful means, working within the democratic system. In retrospect, it appears that efforts of this kind reached their culmination in August 1963 in the famed March on Washington, when whites were still welcomed by blacks as necessary and helpful participants in their struggle to secure civil rights for the black population. Suddenly the situation changed as a new and more fiery generation of young black leaders appeared, proclaiming a doctrine of "black power" and urging blacks to go it alone. They sneered at the little they said had been achieved and argued that the time had come to eschew the policy of nonviolence that had long been advocated, and previously used so effectively, by Martin Luther King.

About the same time young white students, who had been made aware of other blemishes in our society as they worked with blacks to help them gain increased opportunities for self-betterment, found other causes to claim their attention. Increasingly disenchanted with their ability to effect significant changes by nonviolent methods, they also became more activist. A "new left" movement, bent on transforming every aspect of our society, began to form in the United States, in connection with which, in the summer of 1962, a group of college and university students established a new organization: Students for a Democratic Society. Those initiating this movement seem at the outset to have been motivated largely by old world socialist and earlier American populist ideas and to have been strongly opposed to the use of violent methods to effect social change. Their avowed purpose was "to replace power rooted in possession, privilege or circumstances by power and uniqueness rooted in love, reflectiveness, reason and creativity." This perfectionist declaration had considerable appeal for many young people, but, unhappily, the new organization's devotion to relatively moderate goals and peaceful means proved short-lived.

Clear evidence of a changed mood among students, in

which they were no longer to be willing to limit themselves to peaceful demonstrations, appeared on the academic scene with the eruption of the Free Speech Movement on the Berkeley campus of the University of California in 1964. The immediate provocation was an attempt by the Regents of the University to prohibit solicitations for political causes or civil rights issues on the campus. At a time when increased freedom was being experienced in every aspect of our culture, this represented to many students an intolerable infringement of their rights, with the result that the proverbial all-hell broke out, and a new and increasingly violent chapter in the ongoing story of student behavior, and of campus disturbances, had begun. In the next few years demonstrations and violent disruptions for a variety of causes were to spread from campus to campus across the country and around the world.

No fully convincing explanation for this phenomenon has yet been given, or perhaps ever can be given, for various often conflicting forces were at work as the disruptions spread. I am sure that many comparatively innocent participants were drawn into the movement for defensible, perhaps even praiseworthy reasons. But quite early leadership was seized by a new breed of campus radicals for whom it was and is difficult to feel much sympathy. Whatever their motivation, they behaved very much as power-hungry zealots, insensitive to any claims outside their own obsession, have always done. Though they could not understand our reasons, some of us found great similarity between them and the extreme rightists who had caused the earlier disruptions of academic life. They were in fact no less intemperate or any less committed to a conspiratorial theory of society than such extremists as the founders of the John Birch Society. They differed only in that, whereas the Birchers professed to see a communist conspiracy engineered from the left, these zealots beheld a conspiracy formed by a "power elite" on the right that controlled all the institutions of our society, including the colleges and universities. The members of this elite, they maintained, kept the people enslaved and operated the nation's institutions for their own selfish ends. Hence the need, among others, to destroy the existing universities and create "free" ones.

For the New Left the enemy was the "Establishment" created by these elite conspirators, and the goal of social action had therefore to be, not the correction of existing inequities in American society, but its total destruction as a necessary preliminary to building a new order worthy of free human beings. The leaders of the movement felt themselves to be the vanguard of a real revolution. Gaining inspiration from various Marxist writers, especially perhaps from Mao and Marcuse, they looked on the aims and practices of such early heroes of the reform movement as Martin Luther King with contempt, holding them to be ineffectual and naive. Certain in their new faith, they openly and proudly threatened all existing democratic institutions, shouting that the times called for direct violent action; and, carried away by their own rhetoric, rushed on, spreading turbulence and destruction on campus after campus, and elsewhere, in the name of liberation.

If the McCarthy era was a "scoundrel time," so was this; and its saddest feature was that in this instance the attacks on the colleges and universities were contrived and mounted very largely by their own people. It can be said in defense of the academic communities that the attention and support the radicals received within them owed less to sympathy with their ultimate goals than to the ability the leaders among them had to exploit existing sources of discontent, chiefly the frustrations, discouragements, and hostilities bred in our society by our military involvement in Vietnam, which grew steadily from 1965. One way or another, through a combination of intent and circumstance, this new breed of scoundrels gained a hearing with their contemporaries, and, with their ranks swelled, in the later 1960s turned on those imagined creatures of the Establishment, the very colleges and universities which had nurtured them, and on campus after campus occupied—or, as they would say, "liberated"—buildings, threw their rightful occupants out, demanded, marched, smashed, and destroyed with such vocal shrillness, vehemence, and brutality that for a few years normal academic life was brought almost to a standstill.

It seemed to me incredible at the time, as it still does, that educated people, old as well as young, under pressure chiefly because of anxieties caused by the war, could come to look upon our national government and

many other of our institutions, including colleges and
universities, admittedly blemished as they were and are,
as hostile organizations, as "the enemy," and believe
that they were nothing but servile creatures of a wicked
Establishment repressive of human advancement. It is
impossible now to tell how many, or how seriously any
actually believed such allegations. But some did. They
pointed to "the governmental-industrial complex" of
which President Eisenhower had warned, which in their
imaginations had become a monstrous grotesquerie, as
the villain and asserted that the colleges and universities
were a willing and active part of it. They had been
established to serve the truth, but were in fact controlled by and slavishly served the nefarious purposes of
this monster. Perhaps the radical leaders less believed
such extravagant statements than used them in an excited time to influence the gullible; it depends how
cynical one considers them to have been. But, as I have
said, some did so believe, and at a lamentable cost in
turmoil, destruction, recrimination, and hate, as reason
and civility gave place to threats, demands, and violence. The details are a matter of record and need not
be recounted here. My principal personal unhappiness
in all of this sprang from the fact that members of faculties often seemed less mature than the majority of students in their readiness to accept contrived student
protests at face value and to encourage misdirected
demonstrations rather than to stand firm against them.
It is one thing for academics to defend freedom of in-

quiry; it is quite another for them to support or condone acts of violence, however noble the reasons professed to excuse them.

These two principal attacks on colleges and universities—first from the outside, from the right; then from the inside, from those who professed to represent the left—together with the continuing suspicion visited on these institutions by the more frightened conservatives, posed the most serious impediments to the advance of higher education in the years under review. But a further difficulty must be mentioned. This is the worry produced by the steadily increasing involvement of these institutions with the federal government and their mounting dependence on federal funds.

During the war years the colleges and universities had willingly, even gladly, turned from normal peacetime activities to devote themselves as best they could in a variety of ways to national service. With the return of peace many within these institutions felt that the time had come to break away and again pay undivided attention to more proper, long-range educational objectives.

A related issue that divided individuals within the academic community as the war ended was the attempt to establish a national program of peacetime compulsory military service. Many senior officers in the armed services, as well as some older men among college and university administrative officers, members of Congress, and others from the general citizenry who had participated in the First World War, and whose impressions formed in that period had been reinforced as they carried out important responsibilities in the Second, felt strongly that steps should be taken to ensure that the nation would never again be drawn into war unprepared. Toward that end they undertook a determined effort even before the war had ended to have a federal law enacted to make military training compulsory for all young men in the future. As such a program would be directed primarily at eighteen-year-olds, it could not fail to have a disruptive effect on college enrollments.

The latter prospective consequence undoubtedly explains some of the fierce opposition the proposal stirred up in academic circles, but not all of it. I am confident it owed more to a basic disagreement about the best kind of education to produce self-reliant citizens for the service of democracy and the most promising way to ensure the nation's safety. Opponents of the proposal were convinced that traditional higher education had more to offer toward the achievement of these goals than did military training, whereas proponents were just as convinced of the contrary. The college communities produced articulate spokesmen for both sides in the public debate of the issue which immediately erupted, and feelings ran high. Gradually the arguments of those in opposition prevailed and the attempt failed. However, a compromise Selective Service Law making men aged nineteen to twenty-five subject to draft was enacted in 1948. (After the outbreak of the Korean War the age limits were lowered to eighteen and raised to thirty-five.) This law provided a system of deferments favorable to college students and to others who chose to continue their education in areas considered to be of strategic importance for the nation's defense. At the time such provisions seemed quite sensible and in the nation's best interest, but later, in the period of the war in Vietnam, they engendered a new set of controversies as doing violence to democracy by giving advantages to those who went to college which were denied to those who did not.

In the early postwar period, after the attempt to enact a compulsory military service measure had failed, the number of Reserve Officer Training Corps units on college and university campuses was increased substantially. This program provided an acceptable way of attracting college men with leadership potential into the military services; from the colleges' viewpoint it promised to help keep enrollments up in what were expected to be lean years before the population bulge reached the college level. Furthermore, these units gave the students who joined an opportunity to discharge their military obligation without interrupting their education. It is not surprising, therefore, that they were sought after by many institutions, and where awarded, were welcomed by administrators and students alike. It is a commentary on how suddenly and violently public opinion can change in our society that later, in the period of violent student protests during the war in Vietnam, these ROTC units became targets of strident student and faculty resentment and were often decommissioned as eagerly and joyfully as they had been set up only a few years before.

Differences of opinion and worries over national policies and the proper relation between institutions of higher education and agencies of the federal government were not confined to questions of the military service to be required of young men. (Nothing was said about service duties for young women in those days.) Agencies of the federal government which had turned to the colleges and universities for help in carrying out their missions during the war years continued to do so in the immediate postwar years, and it was not long before others adopted the practice. The educational institutions seem not only to have responded favorably when invited to continue contractual arrangements with these agencies, but in many and a growing number of cases eagerly and actively to have sought to widen and extend such involvement. Such readiness on the part of the educational institutions to assist the federal agencies may well have owed less to patriotic resolve than to the advantages federal dollars brought to the institutions and their people, and to the opportunities they often provided the institutions, directly or indirectly, to strengthen existing programs or establish new ones. However this may have been, in all of these contractual arrangements there was an area of mutual interest: the government was aided and the educational institutions were strengthened. The result was that the numbers and magnitude of such programs grew steadily until, as we have seen, in the case of the large research universities, programs supported by federal funds came to constitute a very considerable part of their activity.

But from the very beginning, as indicated in my second chapter, such arrangements occasioned some anxiety. A principal source of worry was awareness that there was a serious risk in becoming dependent on federal dollars which could be cut off at any moment. Yet it is my recollection that Harvard alone among universities entering into research contracts with federal agencies declined to have any part of the regular salaries of its permanent appointees paid from funds provided by the federal government. There was also concern lest the government have too much to say about what research should be done and lest it restrict the free exchange of information among scholars. In an effort to meet the first of these difficulties many universities insisted that research could be done on their premises only as the motivation for it originated in the normal research interests of one or a group of their own people. But in regard to the second, it is my belief that again Harvard alone refused to permit classified research to be done on its campus, holding to the principle that in peacetime scholars should be free to publish the results of their inquiries and indeed that, for the sake of the advance of knowledge, these should be made available, without restriction, to anyone interested.

There were numerous other grounds for concern in the large involvement that was developing on the part of the institutions of higher education with agencies of the federal government; and repeated discussions of what the proper relation between them should be began quite early. An early example was the meeting arranged by the American Council on Education between educators and representatives of the Department of Defense and of Selective Service in July 1950 to address such questions as: What role should the colleges and universities be expected to play in national defense in time of peace? Was this a time of peace? How far could an institution go in accepting money from the federal government without the government's beginning to determine or at least to influence—possibly also to distort— policy within the institution? How far are the aims and purposes, more particularly the immediate concerns, of the federal government compatible with the basic purposes and long-range responsibilities of colleges and universities?

These were some of the questions raised, and misgivings felt, from the very beginning. Harvard had one of the first internal studies made to determine what effect the new development was having on its activities in 1959. But since the advantages to the institutions clearly seemed to outweigh whatever disadvantages were experienced or feared, until near the end of our period, when changed circumstances put the whole matter in quite a different and may I say highly prejudiced light, expressions of discontent were restrained and the involvement continued to grow. Yet doubts remained, and to the old ones new ones were added, especially from the late 1960s when all institutions receiving any federal funds were required to develop programs of affirmative action to increase, first the number of blacks, and very soon of women, in their employ, under penalty of losing those funds. The quarrel was with the means rather than the ends. Especially resented was the enormous increase in paperwork, with its concomitant multiplication of expense, to which they were subjected in order to provide the information required and to feel confident that they had complied with all of the provisions of the many governmental regulations. There was mounting evidence that the educational institutions, even the so-called "private" ones, were losing the privilege of controlling their own affairs.

One might ask why I have introduced consideration of the new, enlarged involvement of institutions of higher education with agencies of the federal government that developed between 1945 and 1970. The constant criticisms of colleges and universities by conservatives and liberals, and especially the attacks on them by reactionaries and radicals, made progress difficult. On the other hand, increased involvement with the federal government played a major role in making possible the unprecedented advance in higher education which occurred during the period, which this book celebrates. Why, then, bring it in here? Simply because, helpful as it undoubtedly was, and is, it contains worrisome elements, which, in my judgment, have worked against optimum advance of the higher learning. There are reasons why academics, intent on their own intellectual aims, should share the conservative distrust of big government.

It is a source of regret to me that the story of the great development of higher education toward which I have sought to direct attention could not be told as one of unimpeded advance, but it could not in truthfulness be so treated. There were a good many roadblocks along the way, the most distressing in my opinion the campus disturbances that erupted toward the period's end.

In considerable part as a consequence of the difficulties visited upon colleges and universities at that time by their own people, the fortunate environmental circumstances that had earlier provided the incentive and the numerous opportunities for growth and new departures and furnished the means suddenly very largely disappeared. Though it is my principal thesis that it would be a miscarriage of justice if, in major part because of the extensive and lurid publicity given them by the media, these difficulties were permitted to obscure the great accomplishments of the period, it cannot be denied that it came to a confused and dispiriting close. In the face of these difficulties, factions and rivalries developed within and among departments and faculties within institutions, and because of the disagreements and ensuing animosities, it became virtually impossible to find grounds for common allegiance or to obtain consensus on policy issues.

Meanwhile, responding to pressures from students in many institutions, requirements for degrees were relaxed, in some instances even eliminated. Formal courses were frequently replaced by individually initiated programs of study bereft of any organizing principle. Number or letter grades gave way to indications of pass or fail, or to no grades at all. Attempts to define specific content for either general or professional programs of study, or to prescribe core curricula, were abandoned. And any lingering sense of participating in a common undertaking, and guiding it, which presumably to a degree members of faculties had once held, was seriously weakened if not completely lost.

At the same time costs had come seriously to outstrip income. Public interest in higher education had lessened where it had not turned actively critical. Everywhere retrenchment was called for. In the midst of all these difficulties faculty morale sharply declined. For the moment there was little evidence of cohesion within the enterprise on any campus, or any discernible agreed-upon goal or sense of direction. There were substantial grounds for despondency, and this despite the fact that in my view, my recurrent theme, American higher education had just enjoyed its most fortunate period, one in which the whole enterprise had prospered as never before and in which our leading universities had set a new and higher standard for the world.

Clearly one period had ended and another, more difficult one, had begun. But the institutions had survived. They continued to function and their fundamental character remained intact. Moreover, though the prevailing mood within them was less expectant, considerably more somber than it had been twenty-five years earlier, they had begun to demonstrate impressive resilience. A new beginning was being made. Presidents and other administrative officers, confronted with this sudden and sharp reversal of fortune, were busy seeking ways to bring budgets into balance. Faculties, collegiate and professional, were beginning to put aside or moderate their internal dissensions and, with attention redirected to their primary responsibility, to ask again what purpose or purposes higher education had been instituted to serve. Everywhere they were seeking to define anew what the degrees they offered should or could be made to mean, and what those who were awarded them could be expected to know.

In the light of these developments, it seems likely to this observer that the story of growth has not ended, that the losses suffered during the recent brief time of troubles will soon be made good, and that advance can begin again from the highly advantageous positions won during the previous quarter-century and, for the most part, made secure.

5

·O·O·O·O·O·O·

Aims

What, during all this development, while we were so busy reacting, did we *think* we were doing? For we did repeatedly, some of us perhaps almost continuously, try to find theoretical justification for our behavior.

At the outset of the period under discussion two reports attempted to reformulate goals for higher education. These documents, though now perhaps generally forgotten, were widely read and discussed at the time of their appearance. They foreshadowed a basic difference of opinion about the proper primary emphasis in higher education that was to recur again and again throughout the debates concerning the purpose of higher education that took place during these years, and persist beyond them.

The first was the Harvard report, made public in July 1945 before the war had ended, entitled *General Education in a Free Society*. It was produced by a committee appointed by President Conant during the war years to reflect and report on what kind of education schools and colleges should seek to provide in the United States when a new beginning could be made at war's end. As in part a kind of panegyric on democracy, the report anticipated the optimistic and adulatory view of democracy that was a marked feature of the early postwar period. To this extent it was a product of its time, so it is perhaps not surprising that from our present perspective much of what it said seems considerably outmoded. But when it first appeared it met with a great deal of interest, if far from universal approval, and unquestionably influenced both substantive policy and nomenclature. Certainly it gave wide currency to the term "general education."

Some readers saw in the use of this expression only a misguided striving for novelty, holding that it was nothing more than an evasive name for what had always been called liberal education. This criticism resulted in part from the fact that those who made it failed to read the report in the Harvard context. Had they done so, they would have realized that the general education proposed in this report was intended to provide only a part, not the whole, of undergraduate education, to say nothing of education at the graduate and graduate-professional levels. Harvard's program of education for undergraduates had for a long time consisted of three parts—concentration, distribution, and the benefits that came from extraclassroom activities in a residential college—and it was anticipated that this would continue. There was no disposition to abandon the concentration requirement (referred to in most institutions as the requirement of a major) under which each student was obliged to take a number of courses in a specialized field. General education was offered simply as an alternative, or rather as a more carefully articulated program, to meet the earlier distribution requirement.

But for the report's authors, as for many others, if the term they introduced did not bespeak an entirely new conception, it did denote an important new emphasis. If nothing else it implied that there was a definable kind of education that could be distinguished from every kind of specialized education that had goals and aims of its own. Its advocates went further and insisted that this kind of education, though it might find expression in different ways, had universal applicability for all educated people, and that it therefore deserved to be pursued by, indeed should be required of, all students for its own sake. The point of view set forth in the Harvard report was not as novel as it appeared to many at the time, for its general thrust and many of its specific prescriptions had been anticipated at Columbia and on other campuses where somewhat similar experimental programs had been introduced in earlier years. But incentives for college faculties everywhere to devote increased attention to general education were greatly strengthened by the Harvard endorsement, and soon, however differently they interpreted the expression, there was scarcely an undergraduate college of liberal arts, or a college of arts and letters in a university, that did not boast that it offered a program of general education.

Insofar as its primary concern was for the individual,

the Harvard conception of general education followed in the liberal arts tradition. But there were departures that perhaps warranted the introduction of a new term, an important one being that in this report the individual was seen as living in a particular kind of society. As President Conant, quoting the report itself, expressed it in his President's Report for 1949: "General education looks first of all to a student's life as a responsible human being and as a citizen." The report stated more precisely that the chief business of schools and colleges is to provide a kind of education suitable for free men, that is, for men (and women also, though in the 1940s no need was felt for any such explication) who lived in a democratic as opposed to a totalitarian society.

The report followed tradition in stating that what is needed is an education that will teach or rather help young people to learn "to think effectively, to communicate thought, to make relevant judgments, and to discriminate among values." But it went beyond when it added an explicit statement that such education rested upon the attainment of an understanding and appreciation of the Western democratic heritage. Here the influence of the war was obviously felt. The report recommended the establishment of core curricula for schools and colleges that would include study of great texts of literature, basic science, and mathematics and, along with these, Western thought and institutions. The purpose of introducing the latter requirement was to increase understanding of and allegiance to the free society of the report's title by the production of enlightened free men. The society the authors had in mind was clearly Western society as it was understood to have developed since the Renaissance and had been defended in the war—perhaps more specifically, as the culmination of this development, the contemporary American society with its democratic form of government.

For purists among defenders of liberal education in academic circles even this much concession to social considerations in the design of a program of education to produce free individuals represented the beginning of a fall from grace. Others felt that the Harvard report paid far too little attention to social needs. These critics were inclined to excoriate it as being excessively historical, backward-looking, traditional, conservative, and narrow. Time would support some of their charges. The report's confident understanding of Western values came to be challenged. Its emphasis on Western civilization, with comparatively little attention to non-Western cultures, quickly came to seem too restricted. Its concern for history appeared excessive as other methods of inquiry came into favor and were increasingly employed. It accorded far too little space in its scheme for the study of science in view of its important and shaping role in modern culture. This undervaluing was even more serious in the case of the social sciences. A few held from the beginning that the report's understanding of the place of the study of religion in higher education was unsympathetic. But in a fair appraisal the report could not fail to be seen as both timely and helpful, and as thoughtful, generous, and humane. I call attention to it here as an example of a careful and influential attempt to update and adapt for the new time, aims and practices which had long been observed in higher education and had proven their worth, but which were to be increasingly challenged in the years ahead, until some of their adherents would come to feel—I consider mistakenly—that if they had not been completely deserted, their alteration had been so extreme as to have produced virtually the same result. But more of this later.

The second report, that of the National Commission on Higher Education appointed by President Truman in July 1946, differed sharply from the Harvard report in both tone and effect. George H. Zook, who had been prominent in higher education throughout the years of the Roosevelt administration as a staunch advocate of liberal causes, and who at the time was President of the American Council on Education, was made chairman of the commission. Its report, forthrightly entitled *Education for American Democracy,* was published in December 1947.

Just as the authors of the Harvard report had done, Zook and the other members of his commission saw the world divided between democratic and totalitarian regimes. But starting from this agreed point they were thereafter less concerned with the advantages provided free men by the democratic form of government than with what they held to be the "equalitarian spirit of the American heritage." They were less interested in the development of individuals than in social advance. They were also more interested in the future than in the past and had much less to say about the virtues and achievements of democracy than about its unfinished tasks. For they believed that to preserve and defend democracy it was necessary to improve it, and they had no doubts about how this was to be done.

They conceived of education primarily as an instrument for social change and held that a primary purpose for it must be to effect the equality for all American citizens that was already prescribed by law. They echoed the Harvard report in making a strong plea for general education, but held a different view of what this implied. For them general education was "liberal education with its matter and method shifted from its original aristocratic intent to the service of democracy." It has always been curious to me how frequently this charge of aristocratic exclusiveness has been repeated by self-consciously liberal critics of American higher education who persist in ignoring the numbers of poor young men for whom it provided an avenue for career advancement in every earlier generation. But the charge is easier to understand today when the conception of equality has come to admit of no distinctions.

The members of this commission argued that every young person should have the opportunity for at least two years of education beyond high school. They did not mean quite everyone, but they cited statistics to demonstrate that 49 percent of the age-group had the ability to do academic work at this level and called for the establishment of tuition-free community colleges to meet this need. Their report dealt at consider-

able length with the economic barriers that limited access to higher education. It opposed discrimination of
all kinds, speaking out especially sharply against racial
segregation. It predicted there would be 4,600,000 students (including 600,000 graduate and professional students) enrolled in higher education by 1960. These
figures seemed astounding at the time, but in the event
they did not prove far from the mark. Enrollment fell
short of the number predicted in 1960 by nearly a million, but not for long. There were five million students
enrolled by 1964, and their numbers continued to grow
until by 1970 there were eight million. Today there are
more than twelve million.

For the members of this commission the principal aim
of higher education was to prepare individuals to participate intelligently in community life and public
affairs. So far as education addressed itself to individuals,
its function was to help them to understand their society
and to inspire in them passionate loyalty to democracy
in egalitarian terms. The Commission held that teaching and learning had to be invested with public purpose, and private careers and social obligations made to
mesh. The essential task of higher education was to inspire young people to take a socially responsible and
productive part in the world of work. It is not surprising that their report had comparatively little to say
about classical literary texts of the Western world, for in
their opinion reading books, without at the same time
participating in active, socially significant experience,
had little contribution to make to the desired result.

But they had no parochial view of what was involved, for they went on to urge that young Americans should be prepared for world citizenship since it had become necessary fo us to fit ourselves for world leadership. Clearly they were making no small plans.

There was a great deal more to the report, much that was timely and commendable along with other prescriptions that many found misguided. It made a strong plea for increased attention in academic curricula to peoples and cultures outside Western civilization, especially to those of the Soviet Union and the Orient. It called for the development of interdisciplinary studies and enlarged support for graduate study. It urged the establishment of enlarged and improved counseling services to help students to learn and to make rewarding career choices. It stated that higher education should pay more attention to social invention, social technology, social science, and social engineering. It advocated the addition of more vocational programs, especially in the health fields, along with a continuing survey of the nation's health needs and regulation of the numbers of students permitted to enter professional fields. The report also made a strong, and what was at the time a very bold, call for federal aid for higher education, stating that the federal government should provide scholarships for at least 20 percent of all undergraduates, fellowships for graduate students, and funds to the states to make the desired expansion possible. Finally, in a burst of rhetorical fervor, it called on everyone to work "quickly to make the understanding and vision of our most farsighted and sensitive citizens the common possession of all our people," and closed with the resounding affirmation, "It can be done!"

Well, it hasn't quite. But this report exerted a strong, continuing influence during the period under review—considerably stronger, developments would show, than that of the Harvard report—as much of what its authors aspired to was achieved.

Such were some of the contrasting thoughts in educators' minds as they turned from the interruption of the war to renewed effort in their profession. Some of them looked back longingly to the tradition of liberal education, to the heritage they knew and loved. These were inclined to stress the importance of theoretical, literary, and historical studies. The most extreme among them would have been happy unashamedly to inhabit a reconstituted ivory tower. Others, conceiving of education primarily as a tool to effect social change, looked ahead impatiently, eager through education to create a better and a more just world. These tended to have a more practical orientation, to care more for science and to expect more from it, and to be more interested in contemporary issues and emergent social opportunities than in past achievements. When among themselves the members of this persuasion usually referred to the views of the others disparagingly as being precious, elitist, visionary, and impractical; later they would say, not relevant. The others in their turn held that the ideas of their critics, if put into practice, would erode standards, destroy quality, and condemn the whole enterprise of higher education to mediocrity. Both groups, however, remained polite in each other's company, and it could not have failed to be clear to an outside observer that both placed a high value on education, wanted better education, and according to their lights remained intensely loyal to it. For the moment, all those involved were too happy to be able to return to the practice of their profession to have any desire to engage in acrimonious quarrels with colleagues. And before the early euphoric mood had passed, the pace of advance had become so rapid, and the demands on everyone so pressing and unrelenting—indeed so absorbing—that for a considerable time there was little opportunity or incentive for much theoretical disputation about the exciting enterprise in which they were all engaged. But differences of opinion remained.

There were differences of opinion between those who undertook to speak for colleges and those who spoke for universities, and between and among members of both groups; between those whose absorbing concern is undergraduate education and those preoccupied with graduate programs; between the faithful advocates of unsullied liberal education and those in professional schools; and between those who staunchly asserted the priority of general and those who no less firmly defended the superiority of specialized education. These were only a few of the more readily recognized grounds for division within academic communities. They not only separated kinds of institutions, but frequently existed even in small departments within institutions. In fact, it is in faculty meetings devoted to discussions of the goal of the corporate enterprise and the appropriate programs for reaching it, above all, that one can see why professors have long been defined as individuals who think otherwise. And as if the discordant views expressed by members of the academic community were not themselves sufficient to confuse understanding, similarly conflicting views were repeatedly advanced by others—parents, future employers, preachers, public servants, candidates for political office, journalists, numerous kinds of self-appointed "opinionmakers"— who did not hesitate to instruct members of the academy concerning their responsibility and the proper method of discharging it.

Before going further let me remind you that the expression "higher education in the United States" is a very high abstraction, that back of it one must see more than three thousand institutions—colleges and universities, community colleges and professional schools, technical institutes and other kinds of associations for educational purposes—of different sizes, with different aims, and of varying degrees of strength. More than ten million students, with greatly divergent goals, are enrolled in them and their efforts are stimulated and guided by a half-million faculty members who, no less than the students, exhibit a bewildering array of talents, interests, levels of competence, and range of concerns. Thousands upon thousands of formal courses are offered in almost every conceivable subject or field of study, with a variety of purposes in mind. Learning goes on in classrooms, libraries, laboratories, workshops, theaters, museums, residential buildings, on playing fields, on and off campus, at home and aboard. In most instances the environments themselves, with their traditions, mixtures of people, and peer groups, contribute importantly to the learning experience. With this in mind, and remembering the diversity of interests which motivate those many also on the outside who seek to influence the enterprise, one should not find it surprising that no one has yet been able to give a single, universally accepted definition of what higher education is or should be trying to do, no more in the period with which we are concerned than in any earlier time.

But with so much by way of caveat, now let me turn to the question I proposed earlier: what views did those of us who were involved between 1945 and 1970 hold of the overarching purpose of higher education? Or, put more simply, what did we think we were doing? In my view, as has been implied, the answer must be, a number of, even a number of contradictory, things.

All but a very few, scornful of any concession to practicality, agreed that higher education had some obligation to help prepare individuals for careers. Most parents and, however vaguely, the great majority of students have always expected this, and there has never been any serious question about it. Universities were originally established to produce doctors, lawyers, and practicing theologians; they still do, and now also, as the professions have multiplied, engineers, scientists, research workers of many kinds, architects, planners, educators, business executives, managers, social workers—these and others, and at the lower levels of higher education (I hope this will not be taken as an invidious remark) a great variety of subprofessionals needed to operate our technical society. Though this responsibility was recognized, there was rarely any substantial agreement among those active in any field of professional education about how it could most effectively be met.

The more serious, contentious, and widely publicized discussions of the purpose or purposes of higher education, however, continued to be less concerned with its role in preparing individuals for careers than with what else it should do. And in this period, as earlier, such discussions tended to center on two sets of questions, one concerned for the qualities higher education should seek to develop in individuals, quite apart from its role in preparing them for a particular profession, the other with what the enterprise of higher education in its totality might be expected to do for society.

Advocates of all persuasions were agreed that the enterprise had to concern itself in some way with fostering the acquisition of knowledge as a necessary step in the development of understanding. But the question remained, what knowledge? And, as the years went on, fewer and fewer had the courage to suggest a definite answer. So vast had the field of knowledge become that it was impossible to prescribe a specific subject matter for the content of education with any confidence, and so sharp the contending claims for attention among the great variety of offerings that almost no one dared even to say that one thing might be more worth learning than another. Or if he did, it was almost certain that no substantial number of his colleagues would agree with him. As a consequence, early in this period members of faculties came to speak less about specific subjects with which students should be expected to become familiar as a prerequisite for being awarded a degree and instead to state their requirements in terms of the methods by which knowledge is acquired. The new conviction was that it was less important for students to acquire a common fund of knowledge than that they should learn that there are various approaches to knowledge, each appropriate in its own sphere—mathematical and experimental procedures in the physical and biological sciences; analytical, historical, and quantitative techniques in the social sciences; and quite different methods in other fields, especially in literature, philosophy, and the arts— and that they should develop considerable skill in the use of at least one of the methods.

But this development concerns the means, not the ends of higher education. What, essentially, was the enterprise trying to do? Here divisions sharpened. Those whose chief interest was the education of undergraduate students—or perhaps I should say, those among them whose allegiance was to the traditional humanistic disciplines—continued to hold that the fundamental consideration was the effect the educational experience was to have on the individual student. What was it to do to, what change should it seek to effect in him or her?

Thinking exclusively of young people in the period of transition from late adolescence to adulthood, some said straightaway, the purpose is to train minds, to develop intellectual power, to inculcate respect for facts and for logical progression in thought, to lead one to appreciation of objective standards and the attainment of critical ability—above all, to teach precision in thinking and in expression. But others spoke of persons rather than minds. They held that education can be too intellectual, that excessive emphasis on intellection and abstract thinking dehumanizes education and stunts students in their development, that persons are more than minds, and that attention had to be paid to their emotional—some also said, their spiritual—development, to the cultivation of their feelings and their imaginations, if education at any level was to do its work properly.

Those holding the first position generally were apt to be found among the more conservative members of faculties. They supported calls for more attention to basic education and to discipline. They continued to insist on the importance of subject matter and charged again and again that schools and colleges together, succumbing to ephemeral fashionable interests and practices, were failing to educate. The remedy they proposed was to return to earlier practices, eliminate "frills and trivia" from the curriculum, and concentrate on teaching basic subjects. The effective ingredients for education, they said, are demanding curricula, discipline, and the inculcation of respect for learning.

Most holding such opinions had little knowledge of or interest in science and often seemed to believe that most of the shortcomings, and what they considered the lamentable decline in the quality, of higher education were the result of the excessive attention paid to science and scientists in these years and to the disproportionate financial support available for them. They were inclined to speak disparagingly of graduate education because of what they considered the narrow specialization it required, and they deplored the vast increase in research in academic communities on the ground that this had brought about a turning away from teaching, neglect of undergraduate students, and abandonment of the basic educational purpose of higher education. They insisted on the prior importance of teaching and of theoretical studies, and they consistently opposed efforts to encourage students to learn through doing, especially through participating in off-campus activities, holding that the library was the proper place for learning, not the streets. They considered it a betrayal of trust for institutions of higher education to turn from their responsibility to educate in order to help find solutions for current social problems. They were quick to point out that it had not been uncommon in the past for individuals in educational institutions to entertain ideas quite different from those held outside at any particular moment about what should be done in connection with some specific social difficulty, and that time often proved their dissident ideas to have been to society's advantage. They continued to maintain that the proper business of colleges and universities was not to try to solve immediate practical problems but to remain devoted to theoretical investigations and to produce the highly trained individuals who would in their later careers have the understanding, the will, the wish, and the competence to do so.

The view of those whose plea was for greater intellectual rigor, the maintenance of high standards, concentration on basic subjects, and more discipline in education, though held by only a minority of educators during most of the period under discussion, enjoyed a brief period of popular favor immediately following the launching of the first Sputnik. That event occasioned widespread fear amounting almost to panic that the Russians had got ahead of us in training of the young through their employment of more demanding methods while our young were turning soft, and that this posed a threat to our security. There followed a clamor for a return to basic subject matter and increased rigor in education, though even at the time some saw in this nothing more than an opportunity seized by the more conservative to advance their own prescriptions for society and their enduring ideas of what education should be.

The views of those who held that education should address itself to persons rather than just to minds enjoyed greater favor throughout this period. They were concerned for emotional as well as intellectual development; some, who looked for education to produce nothing less than a transformation of personality, were concerned for spiritual development as well. All of these were not indifferent to what was taught, or to how it was taught, but their more frequently and prominently expressed concerns were for such desired results of education as heightened awareness; deepened understanding of self, of the world, and of the human condition; and enlarged capacity for expression, for feeling, and for enjoyment—qualities they felt marked the mature individual and which it was the proper business of higher education to seek to produce in those who experienced it.

From this concern came one of the most significant advances made in undergraduate education in any period. This was in loosening the tight, exclusionary grip the book had held on it from its beginning. For it was only in these years that at long last a recognized place came to be made for the arts in the curricula and extracurricular activities of virtually all undergraduate colleges. In the years before the war only a few avant-garde, experimental colleges (almost all of them women's colleges) had seen any reason to move in this direction. Now, if slowly at first, and against the strong resistance of those devoted to the more traditional views and practices, almost all did. A place was claimed and found in higher education for nonverbal visual and auditory experiences—as time went on, a very large place. Study about and participation in all kinds of artistic activity flourished as never before in and outside the curriculum—in the visual arts, music, writing, the dance, and drama. Everywhere studios and theaters were built and used, as they and their activities came to be considered as necessary in adequately equipped and staffed colleges as libraries, laboratories, classrooms, and the activities associated with them. This development brought with it a long overdue and widely welcomed enrichment of undergraduate educational experience.

Both those whose chief concern was for intellectual discipline and their more liberal humanistic colleagues who were willing, if not always eager, to make a place in their offerings for creative activity and the arts were staunch defenders of "liberal education." Disdaining the world of money-grubbing and practical affairs, and having little concern for social or political issues, they tended to think of liberal education in much the same terms as had Cardinal Newman nearly a hundred years earlier, who, it will be remembered, defined it as "cultivation of the intellect," but understood this in no narrow way. For them, as for him, it implied becoming familiar with "the great outlines of knowledge, and the principles on which it rests, the scale of its parts, its lights and shades, its great points and its little" (a task difficult in his time, and, most would hold, impossible in ours), and from this experience acquiring "a habit of mind . . . which lasts through life, of which the attributes are freedom, equitableness, calmness, moderation, and wisdom." The end of the whole process in his view and theirs was "enlargement of mind" or "illumination" (*The Idea of a University* [London, Longmans, Green, 1947], pp. 90, 107, 111).

What those who thought and spoke of education in this way believed should be gained from the experience of liberal education was such qualities of mind and person as sensitivity to the nuances of cultivated living, increased awareness, critical intelligence, urbanity, concern for others, moral probity, measure, and other similar ones which they felt have characterized human beings at their best in the most advanced periods of civilization. They all relate to individual development, the age-old and the highest purpose for which liberal education exists. The older humanists and their disciples continued to feel that such intellectual and moral characteristics were most likely to be gained from intimate study of literature and history, to which subjects their younger associates were eager to add the arts. Almost all of them opposed, with declining success, changes designed to make education more functional than cultural, as well as the steady tendency to devise curricula of greater contemporary relevance. Nor did they, as a rule, welcome "innovative" teaching practices. Indeed they scorned the word.

And yet some of their number joined with others to foster a very considerable change, which as it progressed appeared to many to work against their basic and very commendable aim. The starting point was the argument that there should be more emphasis on learning than on teaching, that the teacher's proper task was less to impart knowledge than to stimulate interest, arouse curiosity, and foster and guide self-education. This led to praiseworthy efforts on a number of campuses, soon imitated on virtually all of them, to provide increased opportunity and incentive to individual study and exploration. The motivation for these attempts was the belief that the most promising way to get a person to learn, and to acquire a lasting love of learning, is to bring him or her to do some investigating and discovering on his or her own. But increasing efforts to respond to individual differences led to a steady decrease in required studies, and ultimately to their disappearance. Less and less attention was paid to whatever uniformities, shared interests, and common needs may exist among people—in this case, highly educated people—until it almost came to be believed that there were none and that it was therefore the duty of educators, eschewing normative prescriptions, simply to provide a sufficient variety of options to enable each student to go his own way and follow his own special interest or interests as he or she saw fit. In the most extreme instances, which were fortunately few, particularly as the new youth culture gained strength and the more excited young were less and less inclined to heed their elders, students were encouraged and permitted to design their own programs of study and to be their own teachers to such a degree that the venerable tradition of learning, held in such high esteem by the humanists, all but expired.

However, the views of spokesmen for the humanities, whether as understood in the earlier, more restricted sense, or as including the arts and creative activity, were less influential in shaping the development of higher education in this period than were ideas held about its purpose by colleagues who cared less for the past and the finer insights of literature than for peoples and problems of the contemporary world. For these individuals the proper aim was to prepare young people for intelligent living under the conditions of their own time. This meant, chiefly, acquainting them with the social, economic, and political circumstances in which their lives were cast and making clear that these circumstances were not inalterable and that it was a proper role for educated people to work for their improvement. In this opinion, the idea that young people could be prepared for the fullest possible experience of life simply by introducing them, in Matthew Arnold's words, to "the best that has been thought and said in the world" had always seemed precious, and at this stage of history it seemed outmoded and just plain wrong. Institutions of higher education were set up less to foster development in individuals than to meet the broad needs of society. What were colleges and universities doing to help at this point? What should they be doing? Why their persistent reverence for the past? Why don't their people come out of their ivory towers, behold the real world, and find joy and purpose in working in it? Well, one can and did say in response that there are many kinds of shortsighted views. But the matter cannot be left there.

There can be no ignoring the fact that institutions of higher education were set up and are maintained by societies for social purposes, and not primarily for the enjoyment of those who happen to inhabit them at any particular time. They are of course all chartered by some political authority. But even when these facts are acknowledged, room remains for a wide range of opinion as to just what they imply.

A central responsibility that comes to colleges and universities from their origin has already been referred to several times. This is the obligation they are under— or perhaps one should say, the opportunity they are given—to devise and administer courses of study to prepare the many kinds of highly trained individuals—professionals, but now also varieties of subprofessionals, advanced technicians, and, still, educated generalists— that are needed to enable society to function and to grow. This has been a major and recognized part of their responsibility from the beginning. It was given a different turn and increased emphasis during the years of the Second World War when many colleges as well as universities were asked to provide a variety of specialized training programs to assist the war effort; and it continued to gain in importance in the postwar years of ever-increasing dependence on technological advance, and of enormous industrial and governmental expansion.

Two developments in professional education during this period deserve special mention. The first was a marked tendency to lengthen the time deemed necessary for the preparation of various kinds of professionals— doctors, lawyers, architects, scientists, managers, engi-

neers, and all the rest—as more and more intense specialization seemed called for; and, concomitant with this, a
considerable increase in the number of advanced, post-
graduate professional schools. There had been comparatively few of the latter in the prewar years. At the same
time there was a substantial increase in the number of
junior and community colleges, both private and public
but especially public. This was in fact one of the most
conspicuous features of educational development, especially in the 1960s, when a good many of these institutions were established in various parts of the country to
help meet the demand by vastly increased numbers of
students for access to postsecondary education. As a matter of record, a considerable fraction of the increased
number of students was provided for in these institutions, which were designed—especially the public ones—
to prepare advanced technicians and subprofessionals,
but which at the same time constituted an avenue by
which those who were so motivated could gain access to
higher levels of education in other institutions.

The second development was a very sharp increase in
the practice by which institutions of higher education,
looking beyond their long-accepted responsibility to
provide programs of study designed to prepare students
of normal age for various careers, scholarly and activist,
undertook to offer opportunities for study in academic
environments to a broad assortment of mature professionals well along in their careers. It might have been
expected that these institutions would, as they did, make
a large place in their precincts for postdoctoral pro-

grams for mature scholars, especially scientists, to carry on and advance their investigations or to catch up with the latest developments in their fields. This was almost inevitable in face of the rapid growth and mounting complexity of knowledge. But it was not so readily foreseen that universities would move on eagerly to establish a wide range of possibilities for professionals active in other than academic careers to make use of their resources for their own purposes. This was not an entirely new development in this period—it had been anticipated at least as early as the later 1930s when Harvard set up its Nieman Fellowship program for practicing journalists—but it grew so extensively as to appear to constitute a very important and prominent new feature of academic life. The scholarly and the adult world outside were drawn much closer together. Other early examples at Harvard were the program in Management Development, offered by its Business School for midcareer operating executives, and the one that won even greater response, in Advanced Management, designed for executives who were coming into positions of high responsibility at policymaking levels in their organizations.

These were only a beginning. As time went on Harvard developed other programs for labor leaders; public servants at state and local levels; officials in the civil, diplomatic, and military service of our federal government or the governments of other nations; newly elected congressmen and congresswomen; school superintendents and others involved in educational management; parish ministers; doctors and lawyers; architects and planners; health officers (these from memory, and I suspect the list is not complete). Harvard was not alone in this. Provisions of similar opportunities for a great variety of professionals engaged in many different occupations were made by other universities all across the land and came to be accepted as regular and appropriate parts of their activity. And even this was not the whole of it, for colleges as well as universities, for a variety of reasons, began to consider how they might offer programs that would be of interest to or serve the needs of individuals of more advanced age than their customary undergraduate students. Credit and non-credit courses were offered for older people, their own graduates and others, and an amazing variety of programs, held on and off campus and for varying lengths of time, were developed for alumni and alumni colleges. Before the end of the period colleges and universities alike, whether or not they had had any interest previously in seeking to relate their activities to the needs of older people, were busily engaged in doing so, and the field of "continuing education" had begun to flourish as never before.

Back of all these developments one can see the conviction, held by steadily increasing numbers during these years, that higher education was established for the purpose of ministering to the needs of society. For most of this persuasion this meant something considerably more than simply preparing and subsequently aiding the many kinds of professionals needed to man the existing and developing structures of society. There was implied a deeper obligation to defend that society and to work for its improvement.

The majority of those who thought of the purpose of higher education in these terms, when pressed, were inclined to say that its larger aim was to prepare Americans for responsible citizenship. But when this was said, there was little agreement about what it meant. For some, particularly at the beginning of the period, it implied a responsibility to teach the nature and advantages of democratic social organization as it had developed in the United States, though again there were different views as to how this should be done. For some the proper preparation was to acquaint young people with American traditions and with the great accomplishments of the past, while others preferred to emphasize study of our country's current situation, its needs and aspirations, on the unarticulated assumption that such study would inevitably quicken allegiance to those aspirations. Others held that a major purpose of higher education should be to teach not just about American democracy, but about the whole development of Western civilization; for them the subject of chief concern was the "free world." And beyond them were yet others, a small group, who argued that the chief aim should be, by concentrating on international concerns, to prepare individuals for world citizenship. For the more thoughtful members of all these groups the ultimate goal was not just to produce individuals ready to profess allegiance to democracy as an abstraction, but rather courageous and informed men and women who would honor democratic principles in their lives and join with others in the work of democracy.

Two quite different considerations were in evidence here. Some felt the primary need was to devise programs of education that would emphasize ethical issues and so affect the later behavior of those who experienced them as to raise the moral tenor of our society. Others, less expressly concerned for questions of personal morality, preferred to stress what they held to be higher education's first responsibility: to conceive of itself as, and to act as if it were, an instrument to produce social change. For the latter the true purpose for which institutions of higher education were founded was not simply to extol the virtues of and work to preserve democracy, but to advance it or, as the more critical exclaimed, to bring it into being.

Concern that higher education was paying too little attention to ethical matters tended to grow as the period progressed and the media came increasingly to feature accounts of violence, corruption, chicanery, and deceit. As the evidence of moral decline seemed to mount, the more conservative citizens tended to proclaim again with increased emphasis that education had a responsibility to develop "character." Others spoke less of character than of good moral habits or, more specifically, of concern for others, especially the disadvantaged and unfortunate, and of justice and fairness, honesty and benevolence. Such concerns were expressed in the later years with especial frequency in discussions of professional education. Others argued that the aim should be to develop individuals who would have the courage to stand alone if need be and not succumb either to propaganda or to momentarily faddish ideas. There were a few toward the end of the period who, despairing of American society (I shall say more about this in a moment), held that a chief aim of higher education should be to each young people how to cope with failure. Still another few maintained that there was little point in trying to develop moral qualities apart from spiritual and religious concerns, but ardent secularists bridled at every mention of these words, insisting that the only way to effect moral improvement was to make ethical considerations more rational. Though opinions differed as to just what was implied and as to means, most of those who believed that moral concern had to be included in any acceptable account of the purpose of higher education agreed that the end sought was not merely knowledge about moral and ethical values and problems. They believed, or perhaps only hoped, that increased attention to moral dilemmas in all courses of study, general and professional, would influence for the better the behavior of those who took them, for their own greater personal satisfaction and, even more, for wider benefit to society.

For some, less concerned for personal morality than for the improvement of society, higher education's first responsibility was to produce the many kinds of leaders needed in an advanced democratic society for government, business, community service, the arts, and all the rest. But they held that, in addition, the institutions of higher education had also to produce a great multitude of committed and informed followers, a host of uncommon persons, critical idealists, who would work with these leaders to improve society, and who would constitute—I believe, if I remember correctly, in President Johnson's words—"a bulwark of freedom" to protect that society against both threats of subversion and excessive centralized political power. It is my impression that most of us who were involved in higher education in these years more or less took it for granted that we were in our several ways, directly or indirectly, serving this purpose. Nor did we see any need to feel apologetic about what we were doing.

I must now turn to another group for whom this was not good enough: those who were moved more by the blemishes in and the shortcomings of our society than by its strong points. The authors of the Zook report described above were among the first spokesmen for that point of view in this period. For them democracy did not yet exist in the United States, and it was therefore deceitful, no more than a screen for shameful self-interest, to speak about the need to preserve and protect it. Determined citizens were needed, who would work to build democracy, and it was a chief responsibility of higher education to produce them. This meant that the institutions could no longer stand apart, look on, and comment about what was going on in the turbulent world outside their gates. They had to get involved. Their task was not to work to ensure social stability, but to strive constantly to bring about social change. In the opinion of such spokesmen the appropriate subjects for teaching and research in colleges and universities were not ancient happenings or distant cultures but the problems of our decaying cities, of festering urban ghettoes, of poverty, crime, and unemployment, of racial segregation, of child abuse and neglect of the aged, of inadequate housing, hunger, and too rapid increase of population, of ineffective local government and deficient social services, of pollution, waste of resources, and abuse of the environment—these and others. And it was the proper job of the institutions of higher education not just to study these problems and to prepare specialists who might be equipped to do something about them at some indefinite later time, but right now to concentrate their attention, employ their own resources, and strive directly to find solutions for them.

In the face of such claims all the age-old quarrels about what institutions of higher education owe to theory and what to practice flared up again. Were universities to be concerned with knowledge or with useful knowledge? What did they owe to each? In what proportion? Did universities have any business getting involved in action? Of course some of them in this country, notably the land-grant ones, always had been to some extent, but surely this was not their essential purpose? Purists raised their objections, but in these years the tide of educational practice came to run strongly against them.

Prominent among the social ills institutions of higher education were called on to correct was alleged discrimination in access to education or, stated the other way round, it was demanded that these institutions broaden and extend educational opportunity. It has long been my impression that the majority of parents of students—and indeed most citizens generally—have comparatively little interest in the upper reaches of higher education (or in its more esoteric purposes at any level). What they have in mind when they think about higher education is the undergraduate college, and their view of this is of an institution which provides an experience to which an individual subjects him- or herself for a few years in late adolescence as a necessary step "to get ahead in the world." What it offers is the promise of more desirable and better paying employment and presumably, therefore, of greater personal satisfaction and happiness, as these goods are popularly imagined and sought after at any given moment in time. There is of course more to it than that, I suspect, in the minds even of the most philistine; but for many this is what "going to college" is all about. In our period, steadily from the time of the G.I. Bill, more and more elements of the population were determined to have these advantages.

It was argued—unfairly and incorrectly, I believe—that colleges had previously been open only to children in the more affluent and better established families. Now, it was insisted, this had to change. Voices were increasingly raised to the effect that higher education had to be open to all who had the academic qualifications to attend, whether or not they could afford the fees, and especially without discrimination on the ground of race or sex. In time the latter requirements were written into law, but right along the majority of the institutions worked consistently to make their programs available to increasingly diverse populations. Our society seemed in these years almost to make a fetish of "equality," and to some extent the institutions of higher education accepted that it was part of their purpose to help society advance toward this goal, even if it meant, as it did in a few instances, admitting underprivileged students whether or not they had what had formerly been considered the necessary academic qualifications.

Here again dissenting voices were heard. Critics of these developments insisted that institutions of higher education were established to build not an egalitarian, but a good society. Their goal was not social or economic equality but excellence. Their purpose was to add quality to our national life. They were not set up to bring everyone to a common level, but to produce the leaders and the many more highly trained people required to operate our advanced, free, technological society. Those participating in higher education who were of this persuasion resisted every move in the direction of what they referred to slightingly as "mass education," arguing that they served a mistaken and incredibly shortsighted policy. In their view the continued prosperity, in fact the very safety, of the country depended upon the colleges and universities providing the best possible, the most advanced and most demanding, kind of education for the most talented and ambitious individuals; and they saw no way, at least in their institutions, that this could be made compatible with opening the halls of academe to everyone, or even to very many. They had no fear of being called "elitist," for in their view the main purpose of higher education was to facilitate the fullest possible development of the best talents and abilities that are given to a nation, for only as this is done, they repeatedly maintained, can a strong and deserving democratic society, capable of effectively and fully serving human need, be achieved. A perfectionist view? Doubtless; but unfairly rebuked and scorned as heartless, for in the opinion of those who held it, the alternative policy discriminated against the needs and valid rights of the more gifted.

There were other social goals than that of equality, goals concerned with the health and economic betterment of citizens and the general enrichment of the common life, which the more activist-inclined members of academic communities felt should be pursued directly by their institutions. Some colleges and universities were so inclined to move in this direction, especially in the 1960s, that they seemed to their conservative critics to be turning themselves, in Jacques Barzun's phrase, into "public utilities." This was especially true of professional schools where students and faculty were increasingly inclined to move from libraries and studies to participate in a great variety of off-campus activities organized to provide services for the less fortunate members of society or to design programs and effect legislative changes for their benefit. Society did need such help, and it could also be argued that at least up to a point such participation improved classroom activity by stimulating livelier student interest in what went on there as imaginative efforts were made to relate it more directly to what went on outside.

But such practices could become too absorbing, leading to diminished attention to the acquisition of deeper theoretical understanding for the sake of some hoped-for temporary good, and in the closing years of the period a possibly related, very unattractive development brought the whole tendency into disrepute. Attention has already been called to it, but because it constituted one of the most damaging forces opposed to the development in higher education, it must be mentioned again.

It was charged that the efforts colleges and universities were making to increase understanding of contemporary American society and to prepare professionals to work to strengthen and improve it were hideously misdirected. A new race of critics appeared, particularly in the later 1960s, who could see no good whatsoever, nor any promise, in American society as it was then constituted, and who maintained that to work for it was nothing better than evil complicity. For these individuals the purpose of higher education was not to serve our democratic society, but to produce the people and lead the way to destroy it. They professed to believe that American society and its existing institutions, especially its colleges and universities, were hopelessly corrupt. They were the slaves of a baleful military-industrial complex intent upon holding people who should be free in subjection, and they had to be destroyed as a preliminary step to bringing about the revolution—even then beginning, they held—that was to transform society and liberate its people. As far as higher education was concerned, the need was to destroy the existing institutions—burn them down or at least close them up—and set up counter or free universities to prepare and inspire a new race of leaders to break the bonds of the existing repressive capitalistic society and usher in the beautiful new world, presumably with themselves at the head of it. I incurred the wrath of some who thought and wrote in such terms by referring to them as "Walter Mittys"; but I am afraid, hard to believe as it may be, that at least a few of them were in dead earnest. They were not a group remarkable for a sense of humor. Fortunately the period of turmoil they created, injurious as it indubitably was, was short-lived, and their prescriptions for higher education, appealing as they were for a few years to some inexperienced, idealistic students and a few teachers, never won broad favor.

It should now be clear that there were a good many different ideas current between 1945 and 1970 both about what higher education was doing and about what it should be doing in the future. It should, therefore, not be surprising that it both was and remains impossible to advance any universally acceptable statement of either a single all-embracing end higher education was serving in this period or of one it was held by either critics or defenders it should serve. As higher education had developed in America, it had inevitably, and quite properly, come to serve a variety of purposes.

Universities of necessity served more and different goals than colleges; graduate education had different ends in mind than did undergraduate education, and professional than liberal education. Critics and commentators from outside academic communities usually seemed to ignore these facts in urging such partisan views as that pure learning was more to be sought after than useful knowledge, general education than specialized training, philosophical understanding than technical competence, theory than practice, basic research than applied research, traditional offerings than new courses. Most advocates spoke from entrenched positions, long familiar, and rarely if ever revealed any disposition toward conciliation or willingness to recognize that there might be something to be said for some aspect of an opponent's point of view.

By contrast, except for college presidents, the great majority of individuals directly involved in higher education tend to shy away from advancing theoretical explanations of what they are doing, and they continued to do so in this period. There seemed to be a widespread feeling among them that everything that can be said on the subject has been said, many times; and they were therefore usually ready to accept, or at any rate act upon, the view that what was going on in the institutions of higher education was what should have been going on, and that it required no explanation. Furthermore, since it is relatively easy to count the number of institutions, the students and faculty, the courses offered and degrees won, the buildings and other resources available, and the dollars spent and needed, extramural discussions of education tended, in this period of unprecedented growth, to dwell on such quantitative considerations; but not exclusively so.

Nor should it be concluded that because members of academic communities were disinclined in these years to enter into debates concerning the larger purposes of their craft that these were matters of indifference for them. It was rather that having tried repeatedly earlier and failed to convince their colleagues of the superiority of their views, they had come to believe that the best procedure was to go about their work, each as he saw fit, and avoid the acrimony of continued fruitless discussion. Those who have participated in faculty debates concerning the purpose of education will have a good deal of sympathy with this view. My experience, however, has convinced me that academics do and did care about the larger purposes of higher education and that in the period under review, as in earlier times, there was considerable agreement among them about what they were trying to do. I hope, if I now attempt to call attention to one or two basic convictions which I believe were widely shared, I shall be doing something more than airing my own views.

Since education is a process designed to produce learning, and learning is a matter of growth or development in individuals based on increased knowledge and marked by heightened awareness, broadened interests, more penetrating insight, and deeper understanding, most academics seemed to agree that higher education must of necessity be addressed to individuals. Learning takes place in individuals, not in abstract societies. This is not to say that any of us were unaware that education can affect groups, even masses of people. We were only too keenly aware of the power of publicity, advertising, and propaganda to inject notions and evoke convictions. We were also inclined to acknowledge, despite the injury it did to our pride, that influences from the general culture other than those exerted by formal education often had greater effect in determining what an individual valued and what he or she was to become than did our efforts. The point I wish to make is simply that, despite all the services we were called on during these years to perform for government and business, and the amount of attention we found it necessary to devote to society's problems, we did not forget, contrary to what some of our young critics were to say later, that teaching and learning are matters primarily concerned with individuals, and in academic communities are the matters of chief importance.

I think most of us recognized that this imposed an obligation to consider what a person is and to ask how education can most effectively stimulate and assist personal development. I am sure we were aware of the complexity of individual needs and differences and of the problem this poses for education, but very few of us saw in this situation an excuse for ceasing to seek after the qualities, interests, and potentials individuals have in common. Unable as we were to agree on a specific, essential subject matter for almost any kind or level of education, we all knew that subject matter was of crucial importance and that some things were more valuable for study than others. We were also agreed that it was desirable for an individual to become familiar with several diverse fields of knowledge, or perhaps only with the methods by which they were investigated, but that it was essential, if a person aspired to be educated, that he or she acquire understanding in depth of some limited area in the broad demesne of learning, both general and, where applicable, professional.

We all agreed that education had to be concerned with the contemporary world, and that this implied the necessity to acquire at least some knowledge of science and of the methods by which it works. We also agreed that education had to provide many individuals with the special kinds of knowledge and the skills to enable them to pursue various careers. We always hoped that a significant number of them would become so enamored with learning itself that they would choose the career of the scholar. But with all of this, some of us, devoted to the humanities, continued to insist that at some stage of the educational process, probably best at the undergraduate level, all students should also have the opportunity through literary and historical studies to learn of the insights and experiences of some of the race's more perceptive individuals, and of the events and developments by which we have come to our present situation.

It was our conviction that the purpose of higher education must include a determination to offer at some level a wider view of life, and a richer and better one, than is immediately available to a young person at the threshold of adult life from his or her own experience of contemporary culture.

Some one has said recently (I have forgotten who it was), that society has successfully subdued large areas of the university. It is easy, in view of certain developments that took place in universities, to see how one could have arrived at that judgment. But the extent of the alleged victory can be exaggerated. Colleges and universities have always acknowledged responsibility to help meet practical needs of society, and they did in this period. They continued to be interested in finding opportunities for their graduates in that society for careers that promised both useful life and personal fulfillment. And they unquestionably took on more and more varied responsibilities that were intimately related to the world of everyday affairs than ever before. But despite these developments they did not forego their earlier faith and begin to think of themselves as being completely of that world. The academic and practical worlds, though joined, are different; and in these years, as earlier, the colleges and universities—or perhaps I should say their people—continued to feel a need to preserve a degree of detachment from the world of practice, to be able to stand apart from, observe, and reflect on what was going on in that world, and to ask what mind and learning could do to make it better, and more humane. Recognition remained that institutions of higher education should not attempt to perform tasks that society has assigned to other institutions of its creation, that they have their own proper work to perform. Diverted as their attention was by the insistent demands addressed to them from outside, most of those who had found their calling inside these institutions remembered, and acted on the conviction, that their primary responsibility was for learning and scholarly inquiry, and that, though circumstance now called on them to open their doors as widely as possible, they continued to have a responsibility in the world of learning to set and maintain standards. It was their hope that those of whatever age, who spent some time in their precincts and worked their way through one or another of their curricula, would go out from their halls, to whatever tasks they were called, learned, critical, and concerned.

The quarter-century in the history of higher education in the United States discussed in this book began with a feeling of hopefulness and expectation on the part of almost everyone who was involved in the academic enterprise. The war had ended and it had been won. Democracy had been vindicated. A new, challenging era had begun. Guided primarily, and motivated, by the desire to produce the well-educated, inspired, and humane leaders needed in a modern, complex industrial society with worldwide responsibilities, encouraged and aided by public and private interests to do so, and accorded enormous popular favor, America's colleges and universities experienced unprecedented growth, and their activities and practices, measured by any earlier standard, developed phenomenally.

These institutions grew in capacity to serve greater numbers of students than had ever been served before in any nation—far greater in fact than even the most hopeful had thought possible at the beginning of the period. They broadened their curricula and extended their intellectual concern to encompass the whole world. They greatly advanced graduate education. Thousands upon thousands of advanced scholars were prepared, many in fields that had previously been ignored, to give this country resources in trained personnel in far greater measure and variety than it had had earlier or even imagined. They, especially the major universities, experienced within themselves a phenomenal increase in research activity which enabled them to attract investigative talent from many countries, and made our country the leader in research activity and in responsibility for the continued advance of knowledge in the world. Along with the talent they acquired the libraries, laboratories, and other resources that made these developments possible. And they kept alive visions of human potential and of honor. All these things they did, and more, which seem to me to give this period, the years between 1945 and 1970, claim to be considered the most creative yet experienced in the ongoing development of higher education in the United States.

It is my hope that better understanding and fair

appraisal of the many dramatic developments that occurred within colleges and universities during this period will serve to stimulate and support renewed efforts in their behalf.